CATHOLIC CONVERTS
FROM DOWN UNDER
... AND ALL OVER

CATHOLIC CONVERTS FROM DOWN UNDER ... AND ALL OVER

Compiled by Wanda Skowronska

Connor Court Publishing

Connor Court Publishing Pty Ltd

Copyright © Wanda Skowronska 2015

ALL RIGHTS RESERVED. This book contains material protected under International and Federal Copyright Laws and Treaties. Any unauthorised reprint or use of this material is prohibited. No part of this book may be reproduced or transmitted in any form or by any means, electronic or mechanical, including photocopying, recording, or by any information storage and retrieval system without express written permission from the publisher.

PO Box 224W
Ballarat VIC 3350
sales@connorcourt.com
www.connorcourt.com

ISBN: 9781925138856 (pbk.)

Cover design by Maria Giordano, photo by Michel Krokowiak, used with permission from istockphoto.

Printed in Australia

CONTENTS

Foreword	xi
Introduction	xiii
1 Katie's story	1
2 From atheism to Catholicism: the story of R.J. Stove	5
3 From Zoroastrian to Catholic	14
4 What's a Catholic? The conversion of Father Emmanuel Seo	23
5 Always seeking God: a psychologist converts to Catholicism	33
6 Something just out of earshot	43
7 A Muslim becomes a Catholic	60
8 A Lutheran minister's journey to Catholicism	65
9 From Mao to Catholicism: an Australian Chinese convert tells her story	79
10 Remember who you are	89
11 From temples and mosques: once a Sufi, now a Catholic	106
12 From gay Marxist to Catholic: the story of Christopher Pearson	114
13 From Japan with love: how Kanae became a Catholic	121
14 Certainty mattered in the end	126
15 Why I didn't convert to Eastern Orthodoxy: Fr Brian Harrison's story	130

16 Henry's conversion story	142
17 Conversion at the end of the journey	148
18 Ex-communist becomes a Catholic	157
19 On converting from Buddhism to Catholicism: one convert's story	167
20 From abortion advocate to Catholic	177
21 From Judaism to Catholicism: Tom Leopold tells his story	184
22 From the New Age to Catholicism	188
23 JoAnna, a mother of four, tells her story	198
24 A Hindu couple joins the Catholic Church	204
Endnotes	209

While many of the conversion stories appear here for the first time, some are taken from the Australian Catholic publication Annals *where they were first published (with grateful acknowledgement to Father Paul Stenhouse). Some are autobiographical and others are third person accounts.*

All profits from the sale of this book will go to Aid to the Church in Need.

Dedicated to

*All witnesses to Christ
in the Antipodes and everywhere,
and to all who seek the truth with a sincere heart.*

Foreword

Pope Paul VI made a simple observation that, deservedly, is often quoted: "Modern man listens more willingly to witnesses than to teachers, and if he does listen to teachers, it is because they are witnesses." Wanda Skowronska, Australian psychologist, pro-life counsellor and writer who has studied at Melbourne's John Paul II Institute, and whose paternal forebears took part in the long and heroic fight for Poland's freedom, has put together a riveting book of conversion stories. She has conducted in-depth interviews with a score of modern converts, most of them from Down Under, each of whom responded to some form of witness to the faith.

I once did a course on the Psalms under Fr Carroll Stuhlmueller CP. With a doctorate in Sacred Scripture from the Pontifical Biblical Commission in Rome, he went on to write many articles, books and commentaries on the Old Testament e.g., on Isaiah in the new Jerome Biblical Commentary. He became the general editor of the *The Bible Today*. In one lecture on the Psalms, he took up Psalm 24:6: "Such are the people who seek him, who seek your presence, God of Jacob." He said that the expressions "Seek the Lord, Seek his face, Seek his will", or the equivalent, occur 165 times in the Old Testament, and added: "So a Bible believer is a seeker, ever seeking God's will in the forever-changing kaleidoscope of daily events/challenges/problems/upheavals and joys of our lives."

Every one of the 24 modern converts accorded a chapter in Dr Wanda Skowronska's book came across to me as, par excellence, a seeker – eventually a profoundly grateful seeker and finder, but sometimes on their journey, a sad and shocked seeker – when it first occurred to them that their believed Anglicanism, Lutheranism, Buddhism, Hinduism, Judaism, Eastern Orthodoxy, etc, might not be what they had long cherished as the truest religion. Some of their struggles and confusion, and the fear that they will never know the peace of certitude, are preludes to the eventual joy of discovering that the Catholic Church is their long lost home. Some of this brings tears to the eye.

Since my seminary days and over the years since, I have read many fine books of conversion stories but never one with such a wide array of nationalities, religions and professions as this one. There are Anglicans and Protestants, laity and ministers. There are Asians who migrated to the West as Hindus, Buddhists, Muslims and Zoroastrians. There is a Russian, a formerly died-in-the-wool atheistic communist and a Chinese woman indoctrinated under Maoism who didn't know there was a book called the Bible. There are tertiary teachers and ordinary folk. One fascinating convert was once a recognised New Age guru. There is one very engaging South Australian, once a gay and celebrated journalist, Adelaide's bon vivant Christopher Pearson, who wrote brilliant articles for many Australian newspapers and journals. I enjoyed this book thoroughly and was enlightened and moved by many of the first-hand accounts of long-time seekers, who, finally and joyfully, called the Catholic Church home.

Fr Paul Glynn, SM

Introduction

Do conversions to Catholicism still happen? Do they happen in our post-colonial, post-modern, post-post-modern and post-post everything age? Do they happen in our wounded era, inheritor of wars and cultural boredom, when so many ills confront us at every turn and apathy is so inviting? There was a time when people like St Paul got knocked off their horses, heard Jesus' voice, went blind, saw again and changed their whole lives. But that was then, this is now.

Haven't we seen and learned too much in the past century? And truly, are conversions to Catholicism still happening?

The answer is a resounding *yes*. No matter what happens to us, as Aristotle said, "All human beings desire to know." And Saint John Paul II reminded us of what every truth seeker desires to know. He observed – at the outset of *Fides et Ratio* – that the following basic questions echo throughout every human life:

> Who am I? Where have I come from and where am I going? Why is there evil? What is there after this life? These are the questions which we find in the sacred writings of Israel as also in the Veda and the Avesat; we find them in the writings of Confucius and Lao-Tze and in the preaching of the Tirhankara and Buddha. They appear in the poetry of Homer and in the tragedies of Euripides and Sophocles as they do in the philosophical writings of Plato and Aristotle. They are questions which have their common source in the quest for meaning which have always compelled the human heart.

These questions which have always compelled the human heart do not go away. For as long as there are people on earth, there will be a unquenchable desire and nostalgia for the transcendent. We are hardwired to want to know if there is a "Someone" out there who created the universe, and what that Someone is like – who "gazes" at us from another world, who knows the truth about justice and mercy, about our hopes, our loneliness and sufferings. We cannot help wondering about that mysterious being we call God.

During the past century we heard people announce the fact that many had converted to communism, Nazism, and other seemingly triumphant "isms", many of which have by now fallen into the dustbins of history. There were also movements, though perhaps lesser known, *into* the Catholic Church. Despite the harsh scepticism of Western society, despite the Church's numerous crises, it is clear that many people are still responding to the call to search for the truth about who we are and where we have come from; and to seek answers to the perpetual questions that never leave us. One by one, people have set out on winding paths through hazardous terrain and thought, reasoned, agonised and searched their individual ways to a dramatic destination. Conversion is an ultimate expression of freedom of the human spirit. Beneath the grand designs of politics and power, the varied paths of solitary human seeking and finding have continued without ceasing and these soul-changing searches affect a country's inner fabric more deeply than any political policy can.

In case anyone doubts that this movement into the Catholic Church has occurred, let us glance quickly over the names of some converts from last century. Such converts have included homosexual dramatist Oscar Wilde; actor Sir Alec and Lady Guinness; Bengali Brahmin and writer Brahmabandhab Upadhyay; Turkish Muslim *Timo Aytaç* Güzelmansu who after his conversion studied to become a doctor of Catholic theology; Harold Abrahams (who converted from Judaism in 1934 – he had won the 100m gold medal at the 1924 Summer Olympics, on which 1981 film *Chariots of Fire* was based); philosopher B.E. Anscombe; novelist Graham Greene; historian Christopher Dawson; author and Chinese scholar Su Xuelin; American Protestant pastor Scott Hahn and his wife Kimberley and many hundreds of fellow Protestant pastors and friends; diplomat Dag Hammarskjöld; comedian Bob Hope; former abortion advocate Bernard Nathanson; actress Patricia Neal; Lord Nicholas Windsor, son of the Duke of Kent; and economist Ernst Schumacher. Not to mention the conversion of entire dioceses of Anglicans who have of late joined the Catholic Church. These are well-known examples from the 'great' continents, testifying to the eternal search for God.

But what about the not so well known? One might say that it is all well and good to speak of notable figures from the great continents, but what about Australia, that place near the edge of infinity down the bottom of the earth? Does anyone convert from there these days? We know the stories of great Irish missionaries who came, built churches and schools around the country and who converted so many in a pioneering spirit. How can I forget the Brigidine nuns who transmitted the faith to me in my youth and who had us all sing, whether we were of Chinese, Anglo-Celtic, Polish or Hungarian backgrounds, "Hail Glorious Saint Patrick", "Far Away Enthroned in Glory", and songs to various saints, imbuing us with a sense of the mysterious, unseen realities. How can we forget all the enterprising religious orders such as the Missionaries of the Sacred Heart and the Marists, who came on heaving ships, far from their homes to light the spark of Christianity in the southern hemisphere, beyond which there was only Antarctica?

In comparison with stories of conversion from the 'great' continents, it has to be admitted that relatively little has been written of conversions to Catholicism from Down Under, especially in our times. But this is not due to the fact that they are not happening – for even at the edge of the world, they are happening *all the time*

– and in the most unlikely of places, as the following stories will tell. One of our earliest pioneers, Caroline Chisholm, who was known as the "Emigrants' Friend", was a convert. Caroline was born in England in 1808 in an Anglican family and converted to Catholicism through meeting Captain Archibald Chisholm of the East India Company whom she eventually married. During the 19th century, she worked to better the plight of migrants in Australia, particularly unmarried women, and her face appears on the Australian five dollar note. Many years earlier, the Portuguese navigator, Captain Pedro Fernandez de Quiros, thought he had discovered what we know as Australia in 1606, when in fact he had found Vanuatu, and bestowed on this great south land a magnificent name – however far its boundaries might stretch – the Great South Land of the Holy Spirit, *Terra Australis del Espiritu Santo*. Of course, even if Australia had not been called that grand name by de Quiros, the Holy Spirit surrounds us at every turn, in every land, and takes us by surprise. This little volume is a reminder of this constant movement of the spirit, despite the secularism, scepticism and scientific hubris of our age.

People reading these stories might well be reminded of meeting converts or hearing one of their stories – for the telling of conversion stories will never be extinguished as long as humanity survives. Converts will inevitably tell of *that one moment* when their hearts and souls were touched, through dialogue with another, or through seeing something unusual, or finally understanding something which made profound sense; and that this was the turning point in their road to conversion, for it forever changed their lives. While we know the wonderful work of missionaries in the bush and the desert, it is sometimes the very "presence" of Catholics in such ordinary suburban places such as the supermarket, the bus stop, the cafe, public park or hospital, which sparks the journey of a searching soul. Sometimes it is the existence of a Catholic Church in the area where the convert lives which starts the process, as occurred in one of the following stories when, out of the blue, one young woman entered a church that happened to be open and sensed something she had never sensed before. Often it is the behaviour of Catholics, or a question they have asked themselves which triggers something in curious observers that just won't go away, like the young girl who asked "Who is God?", and kept thinking about it all the time. In each case there is a unique path shaped by the Holy Spirit to the answers, the spiritual treasure each person sought.

When these seekers finally decide to convert, some have been quietly baptised as Catholics in various parishes around Australia after a course with the RCIA (Rite of Christian Initiation of Adults). Others, even more quietly, received some catechesis through a priest, friend or neighbour. One elderly man I know – Jack Simonian – got to know some neighbours in his block of apartments in Hillsdale, Sydney, and through his hospitality and conversation ended up converting an entire family, organising a priest to come to teach them. Also in Sydney, a young Chinese man told me he got converted by watching the funeral Mass of Saint John Paul II. He told me this as we stood on the steps of St Mary's Cathedral, conversing after the beatification Mass of John Paul II in 2011. He related to me how he had been an atheist all his life until he watched the funeral. He had turned on the TV "by accident" and was moved so deeply by what he saw – "I knew this was a good man" – that he went to enquire about conversion when the televised Mass was over. It can take a moment, it can take years, but the spark leads seekers on to another soul space.

People often marvel about space travel and wonder when an astronaut will land on Mars. But a more inspiring, extraordinary journey is surely that of the seeker after truth, who not only leaves one country for another but leaves one world for another, often forsaking all he or she has known. What is characteristic of these journeys is that there is no compulsion involved, they are freely undertaken and involve *reason* as well as *faith* as regards the unseen world which surrounds us. Their stories deserve telling and re-telling, for they are many-splendoured celebrations of God's grace.

It is hard sometimes to put such things into words. Some of our inner experiences are inexpressible and exist in a realm of what the poet Rilke calls "purely untellable things". Seemingly out of nowhere the person reflects on the eternal questions, feels nostalgia for the things of God and turns to seek out a way to the answer. And some journeys reach the light of day and reveal the psychological and spiritual forces at work within the individuals concerned as they respond to the compelling questions. In the following pages converts from Down Under open the door to this soul space so that we get a rare glimpse inside a heart, mind and soul.

There are myriad journeys, all intensely personal, recounted here: from Anglicanism, atheism, Islam, Pentecostalism, Zoroastrianism and many other starting points. They are not only from Down Under, but because Australia is part of the wider universe and has not fallen off the edge of the world, some additional conversion stories from other places – from "all over" – have been included. The converts sometimes faced personal hostility around them. They also tell of differing spiritual approaches and sensibilities. There are many forms of spirituality and ways of responding to the truth, according to the temperament and inclination of the person involved. Some stories which follow are autobiographical accounts, some are third person accounts. A few were originally published in *Annals* and are told again here. In whatever way they are recounted, I would like to express heartfelt gratitude to all who shared their stories on the following pages. You are great witnesses to the ineffable, the search for the Divine and your journeys reach out to future seekers.

In many cases I was fortunate enough to meet most of the

converts and to interview them. Others are taken from conversion stories recounted elsewhere. All are inspiring and amazing and reveal the depth of courage, perseverance, at times agony and finally profound joy, which is at the heart of the greatest of all journeys: the interior, mysterious, unending quest for God, each soul's odyssey to eternity.

Wanda Skowronska
17 March 2015
St Patrick's Feast Day

1
Katie's story

Katie grew up in Brisbane though she was born in Sydney. Religion was something not discussed in the home. Katie can remember having short religion classes in a public school each week. But she never owned a Bible and hence did not know much of what it was about. Katie's faith journey began in Queensland and took many twists and turns until she was baptised. Here is her story.[1]

My name is Katie and I am a newly baptised Catholic. However, my faith journey began many years ago.

This journey began in 1997 in Brisbane. I had a new boyfriend called Tim and the time had come to go home to Victoria with him to meet his parents. As we planned our weekend, he mentioned to me that on Sunday morning we would go to Mass. My heart skipped a beat and all of a sudden I became nervous. I had never set foot in a church before, let alone had any understanding of why you went, what you believed or what you did when you were there.

Nevertheless, off I went, nerves and all, and took in as much as I could. There were people touching their heads and chests in strange ways, standing up and sitting down, up and down, speaking words I didn't understand in unison, and singing songs I had never heard. I felt so out of place.

Despite that awkward feeling, I continued to go to Mass whenever we were together as a family, asked a question here and there, and began piece by piece to make sense of it all.

Then in 1998, my gorgeous Tim proposed to me, and we began

planning our wedding, which was of course to be in a Catholic Church. More nerves! Then many thoughts began rushing through my head. Do I belong in a Catholic church? How can I get married in a Catholic church when I don't fully understand what it means to be Catholic? Why is this so important to Tim? I had many more conversations with other Catholics, other Christians, Tim's parents and finally with a lovely man called Father Bill Fuller, a Catholic Chaplain from the RAAF [Royal Australian Air Force – ed]. On our first meeting, I had never been so nervous in all my life, but this meeting became a real turning point in my faith journey. As Tim was in the RAAF and I was becoming a "RAAF Wife", Fr Fuller talked about Christianity as it pertained to our married life, our other relationships and to surviving the pressures of being an Australian Defence Force family. I made the conscious decision at this point that I wanted to keep learning more about being Catholic.

In 1999, we had our Catholic military wedding at the Royal Military College Duntroon in Canberra with Fr Fuller presiding, and it was absolutely beautiful. I was worried that a religious wedding would make my family feel left out or as if they were not able to relate, but Fr Fuller had an amazing way of reaching the hearts and minds of all people. Again, my knowledge and my faith grew.

Unfortunately, only nine months later, my father took his own life, and my world was turned upside down. The physical pain was excruciating but the psychological trauma was worse. Sadly my Christian faith wasn't deep enough to be of any strength to me at this time. I struggled in every way, and felt guilty and devastated.

In late 2000 in Darwin, my pain faded somewhat as we welcomed our precious Emily into the world. Again I found myself back at a Catholic RAAF Chaplain, Father Mick Taylor, this time talking about the meanings of Baptism and answering yet more questions.

The issue that he really clarified for me was that it was OK that Catholics aren't perfect. I had been really struggling with the fact that people could call themselves Catholic and yet behave in a way that was clearly against the teachings from the Scriptures. He also helped me explore the concept of forgiveness. So Emily was baptised, as was our next child Harrison in 2002.

I then decided that if I was going to raise these children to the best of my ability in a Catholic home with Christian values, I had better get serious about learning more. Soon they would be asking me questions and I wouldn't know the answers.

So in 2003 I joined the RCIA [Rite of Christian Initiation for Adults – ed] group at East Maitland. For the first time in my life I began attending Mass regularly and went to weekly RCIA meetings. I learned so much from so many helpful people. I learned about the Bible, how to pray, and what different things meant in the Mass. I went home and discussed it all with Tim, who we could probably call a "lapsed Catholic", and his faith was reignited too.

In 2004 we moved to another State, but my attempts to continue RCIA were short-lived as my initial meeting was very negative. I was quizzed on many Catholic concepts which I answered inadequately, and it was suggested to me that it seemed I was doing RCIA just to get my children into Catholic schools.

I was shocked at the response and left in tears, realising that I wouldn't be welcomed into the Catholic community there. I didn't set foot in a church for the next two years. We had another baby, Campbell, but didn't feel we could get him baptised at that point.

In 2006, we moved to Canberra where Emily started school, and yes, it was a Catholic school called Holy Spirit. We began attending the weekly "Focus Assembly" which was always moving, and taught the children (and me) about the Gospel and Christian living. We became parishioners at Holy Spirit and for the next five years we were members of this wonderful Catholic community. We decided this was the place to get our bubby Campbell baptised.

Again I learned from other parishioners, from my children, their teachers, and from two of my dearest friends who are committed Christians. My best friend had bought me a Bible for Christmas and I began reading from it when I could.

In 2010, I had a miscarriage and [we] also lost Tim's Dad. It was very different for me to be able to draw upon my faith and prayer in these difficult times.

In 2011 we moved back to Maitland. We quickly became part of the St Joseph's community, where the children began school and our fourth bubby Cooper was baptised. I rejoined the RCIA group that I had left all those years before. Although I still had so much to learn, I then knew that I wanted to become a Catholic.

In January 2012 I received the Sacraments of Initiation at St Joseph's, East Maitland. It was a moving experience and I became quite emotional. I somehow felt whole or full, like a part of me had been missing but now the whole puzzle was complete.

My faith gives me such strength: strength in my parenting, strength in my relationships, and strength to face the challenges of day-to-day life, because I know I am never alone, and that Jesus is with me no matter what I have to face.

Not only am I grateful that I was guided by so many different people in my faith journey, but that I am now able to guide my children, and that our shared faith as a family brings us even closer together. I am truly blessed!

2

From atheism to Catholicism: the story of R.J. Stove

Robert J. Stove, a writer, editor and musician living in Melbourne, was an atheist before his conversion to Catholicism in 2002. The story of his conversion draws from a longer first-hand account which Robert gave me permission to refer to after I contacted him. His account recreates the era of skepticism and philosophic scoffing at religion, in which he grew up. (The following account will refer to R.J. Stove as Robert to distinguish him from his father Professor David Stove.) All quotations are from his personal story.

R.J. Stove was born in 1961 and relates that his upbringing in Mulgoa in NSW was predominantly atheist. While his parents had been Presbyterians as children, they shed their religious belief as adults. It seems almost an expectation in our era that religious belief belongs to an earlier, immature phase of life and needs to be shed at some point in adulthood. Such was the agenda of the philosopher John Anderson (d. 1962) as professor and intellectual moulder of other people's lives. Robert's father, David Stove, having been influenced by Anderson, a militantly atheist professor of philosophy at the University of Sydney, became a philosopher and political polemicist who undoubtedly had a great influence on his son. Robert, looking back, in a moving, online account on his spiritual and intellectual journey (to which this article refers), reflects that he finds Anderson's supposed charm and hold on his students incomprehensible. Robert states of the "atmosphere" of his upbringing:

It was a compound of introverted heathenism, dusty second-hand books, long dignified silences, the smell of dry sherry, and a perpetual fog of tobacco smoke. When I read a biography of Sir Leslie Stephen, Virginia Woolf's father, I found the mental climate of Stephen's existence so similar to my own nonage as to be positively scary. It was as if the author was describing my own home life, quite as much as Stephen's.[2]

The influence of John Anderson, however, was profound and led many erstwhile Christians along a long and winding road to atheism, well described in James Franklin's work *Corrupting the Youth: A History of Philosophy in Australia* (2003). Anderson so disparaged those who held religious beliefs as immature and unable to think things out, that nowadays one might see his abuse of power as antithetical to philosophy itself. While he insisted on rational arguments to support his cause, he created a partisan atmosphere, in which philosophers were the only thinkers in the world, and Christians were somehow childish, alien and lesser creatures, ignoring the rich legacy of philosophical and theological thought in 2,000 years of Christianity. Needless to say, the younger Robert Stove, not knowing anything else, imbibed the philosophical *Zeitgeist* of the times. And yet as he grew to maturity in Andersonian times and climes, he recounts that as a young teenager he tried out Anglicanism but says, "I converted to what I imagined was Anglicanism, but what was in fact a creed devoid of any significant religious content whatsoever."[3] For Robert, it was more of a preference, as one might have for Lady Gaga, rather than a soberly thought out conversion. He left the Anglican Church at 18, as easily as he had entered it. As for any notion of what Catholics were or what they believed, Robert says in his own account of his conversion (all subsequent quotations are taken from this account):

Catholicism – when my family thought about it at all – had two negative characteristics that meant more to us than any positive feature. First, it was considered vulgar. Second, it was considered totalitarian.[4]

Robert says that the first aspect was associated with having Irish surnames, procreating abundantly, having little by way of intellectual interests and voting for the Labor Party. He comments "This last was the worst sin of all in my parents' eyes, during the Vietnam War years." As to the second above-mentioned feature, that Catholicism was "totalitarian", Robert's parents believed that "Catholicism was philosophical treason, the deadliest foe of free thought, and a kind of Stalinism mixed with holy water." These views had enormous influence on the young Robert and it was not until he was much older that he could "face down this bogeyman without undue difficulty".

In what must count for an extraordinary irony, the Schoenstatt Sisters, an order of German Catholic origin, happened to be neighbours of the Stoves in Mulgoa, and exerted an influence on the family simply by what Robert calls "sheer goodness-in-action". Not even the Stoves could resist the "something" that the sisters exuded, their witness to a spiritual dimension to life. However, Robert explains that the family came to like the sisters thinking that they were lovely human beings *despite* their religion not because of it, much in the way that a communist might have some redeeming personal features to a non-communist but not represent the creed as a whole. As things turned out, Robert's father even cut branches of his pine trees to give to the sisters at Christmas time. Common human friendliness can cross any boundary.

However friendly the relations with the sisters next door were, this did not dampen the suspicious view of Catholicism as a whole which obviously had a dubious history filled with power-hungry popes and war-mongering armies. With little understanding of the reality of the Church at the time, Robert recalls:

> However dimly and inadequately, I had learned enough Catholic history and Catholic dogma to know that either Catholicism was the greatest racket in human history, or it was what it said itself that it was. Such studying burned the phrase "By what authority?" into my mind like acid. If the papacy was just an imposture, or an exercise in power mania, then how was doctrine to be transmitted from generation to generation? If the whole Catholic enchilada was a swindle, then why should its enemies have bestirred themselves to hate it so much? Why do they do so still?

With many of the prejudices and fears of Catholics as statue worshipping, irrational believers in miracles, Robert says his conversion was still years off. In addition he considered that Catholicism would be a catalyst of lunacy and have deleterious effects on anyone who submitted to its supposed rigidities. He also recalls that the influence of certain Catholics he met at the time was less than edifying and indeed quite a put-off.

It was, however, the effect of two family tragedies that had a more profound inner impact on his life at the time. In 1993, his mother suffered a massive stroke and the person Robert had known and loved was not there in the way that she had been previously. From that point on she needed around the clock nursing care. This coincided with the tragedy of his father's oesophageal cancer and subsequent bouts of mental illness. Robert's father convinced himself that his telling his wife of the cancer had somehow caused her illness and he went into a decline that eventuated in being scheduled and requiring intense mental health care. During this time Robert's father was in deep anguish, seeming to question much of what he had believed in earlier life and wondering at the meaning in his life. He was found by Robert reading a Gideon Bible in hospital at one stage. Seemingly better, Robert's father convinced his psychiatrist to release him, against the better judgement of the hospital authorities. Then an unthinkable tragedy occurred. Within a day Robert's father was found dead – he had hanged himself in his garden.

The impact of this tragic event led to a sense of desolation and soul searching. Robert says of his father's suicide:

> This was in June 1994. I cannot hope to convey the horror of this event. It dealt a mortal blow to the whole atheistic house of cards which constituted my own outlook. Was Dad in hell? If not, did he have the smallest hope of heaven, despite the manner of his death? If so, by what means? How much did my own evil contribute to his suicide? And how could I even begin to make amends? The story of the next eight years, until my own gruesomely belated baptism on 11 August 2002, is very much the story of how I writhed over – and wrestled with – such questions.

Robert, in his restless and agonised state, took to searching for answers to the tragedies he had lived through, seeking meaning and consolation if it was to be found. He began reading widely and among the philosophical and religious books he read were catechetical texts, sometimes entire biographies of Catholic saints and accounts of Catholic heroes. He read several works of Chesterton, Belloc, Waugh, Christopher Dawson, Fulton Sheen, Frank J. Sheed and Arnold Lunn. He recalls, nonetheless that the single most important volume was one given to him by a priest whom he met when he was ill. It was a volume published under the aegis of the Missionaries of the Sacred Heart, *Chats with Converts*, by Fr M. Forrest. Robert does not name the priest who spoke to him in his account – he simply calls him Father X – but sees this priest as an important influence in handing over the volume, outlining the legacy of thought which he could tap into as a nascent convert. It comes across in his own account that in the seclusion of his soul, he experienced something so moving, so subtle and yet so vast, that it reoriented the way he thought. Robert says it is not happy-clappy, holy-roller Pentecostalism approaches that work with converts like himself. No, what he needed was totally different: it was what he calls the "sheer logic of faith". He says the priest who gave him the influential volume somehow seemed to know that in his overwrought emotional and spiritual state it was this sheer logic, what Wallace Stevens termed a "blessed rage for order", which got through to him and spoke to the depths of his mind and soul.

After some time, he comments:

> When in the course of my literary duties I came to learn in depth about two outwardly unrelated 16th century events – the battle of Lepanto, and the Elizabethan martyrs' *via crucis* – I could no longer resist entry into the Catholic Church. In honour of the pope who had done so much to make Lepanto possible, as well as of his 20th century namesake so vilely slandered as "Hitler's Pope," I took Pius as my baptismal name.

Robert states that due to Father X, the course of Catholic instruction he undertook could be described as *Chats With Converts* writ large. Reading it, he saw that it revealed, patiently and elaborately, the infrastructure of what Catholics believe. It also seemed allied with the approach of the volumes well known in the 1940s and 1950s: Fr Leslie Rumble's *Radio Replies* which Robert also read. He says:

> I think Father X knew that to the adult mind – even the adult mind as uninformed on vital issues as was my own – emotion is not enough: it is pitifully, painfully not enough. It can be, to a mind periodically disordered anyway, a

lethal drug. What such a mind needs is a solid diet: neither the thin watery gruel of quasi-New-Age "spirituality", nor the pure tabasco of fire-and-brimstone threats. Those who have had the privilege of reading *Radio Replies* will know how nourishing it is, how fair-minded its author is, and how incapable he is of intellectual sharp practice for the sake of making a cheap point. Those who have not yet read it, are in for a great and sustaining pleasure.

Although the legacy of Catholic thought was resonating with him at a deep level, Robert nonetheless found prayer difficult though not impossible. He is surprised at his own aptitude for the faith, saying:

> I am staggered by those Catholics who saw in my "dry soul" (Waugh's apt words) any seed of potential faith, however tiny. That any Catholic would ever agree to be my godparent astonished me at the time of my baptism, and it continues to astonish me now ... Like most converts, I suppose, I naively assumed that the difference made by becoming a full communicating Catholic would be spectacular. Instead, I found myself in the position of one who, while he has only recently acquired a passport, has enjoyed permanent residence for years.

However, not only was he baptised in 2002 but at the same time Robert became acutely aware of the persecution of Christians in the world seeing it in a broader historical context:

> Come 1999, when the Indonesian TNI exterminated as many East Timorese Catholics as it could, any Australian with the slightest historical knowledge experienced a sense of déjà vu. In the 1920s the main venue for anti-Catholic genocide had been Mexico. In the 1930s it had been Spain. In 1999 it was East Timor.

He was also aware of the unfolding sexual abuse scandals, but realised that these did not speak for the Church as a whole. They merely spoke for those who abused their role within the Church and who did not follow what Catholicism taught. He was reminded of the reality of Original Sin and its effects throughout the ages.

Nor did Robert find his conversion inimical to the intellectual life. He became enamoured of the rich legacy of philosophical and theological thought revealed in the writings of the past 2,000 years, but also by its music. He quickly realised that there were various views on music within the Church – seeing some of the camp song music as an "aesthetical mud bath". Though music was not the primary source of influence in his decision to convert, he did have a special interest in it and, in addition to his writing and editorial work, began composing sacred music. His short choral work, *O Salutaris Hostia*, premièred on 29 May 2005 in San Francisco, and was performed by the Schola Cantorum of the National Shrine of St Francis of Assisi. On the following 21 August, *Tantum Ergo* (a companion piece to *O Salutaris Hostia*) received its première with the St Mary's Singers in Sydney's St Mary's Cathedral. He also composed a short motet, *Ave Verum Corpus* (2009). He has written prolifically for several journals and also a work on César Franck, entitled *César Franck: His Life and Times* (2012), published by Scarecrow Press, Lanham, Maryland.

In the account of his conversion Robert addresses, with intelligence and clarity, any atheists who might be thinking about the Catholic Church and analysing its thought but are put off by the recent scandals. His words on this point are worth quoting at length:

> To any atheist who might still be hesitating upon the brink of converting to Catholicism, understandably shocked beyond measure by priestly sins that cry to heaven for vengeance, I would say something like the following words:

"Those dirty criminals who rightly disgust you: do not think of them as Catholics. Unless they repent (and by now mere private repentance is no longer a legitimate option for them), they will go where St Paul promised that they would go. Think, rather, of the saints ... Compare Catholic saints to even the most scrupulous individuals whom the anti-Catholic world has to offer. How many Gramscis would there need to be to equal, intellectually or morally, one Aquinas? How many Cecils equal one Campion? How many La Pasionarias equal one Teresa of Avila?"

... "Above all: be prepared to have your power of reason exercised, as it has never been exercised before ... If you want arrogance, do not seek out Catholic doctrine. Seek out, instead, the surrealistic nostrums peddled by your local newsagent's weekly rags: salvation through Princess Di; the divinity of Nicole Kidman; Brad Pitt's freedom from original sin. Anyone who's been tempted to worship those strange gods in the past, might well be impressed, not by Catholicism's impudence, but by its modesty."

What detours I might have been spared, had someone spelt these things out to me.

Robert's journey reveals beneath its many detours, a persistent honesty in searching and, beyond the surface of received opinions, prejudices and stereotypes, a profound reasonableness. Like an anchor in the dark questionings and tragedies along the way, this reasonableness led him to be open to realities beyond the visible world, to unimagined places of the soul, to the mysteries of the Catholic faith, to his everlasting spiritual home.

3

From Zoroastrian to Catholic

A young Sydney woman, Khush, describes her journey from Zoroastrianism to Catholicism in the following interview. I met Khush after attending a weekday Mass one evening at St Michael's Church, Daceyville, a suburb in eastern Sydney. The parish priest, Father Jerzy Chrzczonowicz, invited his parishioners into the presbytery for a cup of tea. As Daceyville is not my regular parish, Father Jerzy introduced me to the half dozen or so people who were sitting around the table. When Khush, who was sitting on my right, was introduced to me, it was with the words "Khush is a convert". After greeting Khush, I asked, "What did you convert from?" She replied "From Zoroastrianism". I have to say I nearly fell off my chair as I had never heard much of Zoroastrianism, much less of a convert from the religion of Zoroaster. Thus began a friendly series of conversations and one day Khush was happy to grant me this interview to recount her extraordinary journey to the Catholic faith. The interviewer questions are in bold italics below.

Where do you come from Khush?

I was born in Bombay (Mumbai) in India but have been living in Australia for the past 10 years. My family were Zoroastrian – they are also known as Parois in India. It is a very ancient religion. You know, King Cyrus and Darius were Zoroastrians. However, after the rise of Islam in the seventh century, many Zoroastrians fled from Iran in about 1400AD, as they were persecuted for a long time by Muslims and they made India their home, especially Mumbai. There has been a group of them living in India ever since. [About 70,000 – only 20,000 remain in Iran].

What did you believe, as a Zoroastrian?

Zoroastrians believe in the teaching of Zoroaster, whom they regard as a prophet and who was born around 628 BC. Zoroastrians believe that Zoroaster has revealed the existence of Ahura Mazda to us, whom we understand as the "lord of wisdom", the supreme divine authority. According to the holy book Avesta, Zoroastrians believe that Mazda was filled with a holy spirit. In Zoroastrian tradition there is a good spirit represented by Spenta Mainyu, who is for order and good and an evil spirit represented by Angra Mainyu, who is for chaos and destruction. There will be an end of the world where evil will be purged in heaven and earth, and it is mentioned in the book that the "son of God" will come to the earth.

It is like the book of Genesis, in that there were bad angels who fell away from God and the good and bad angels are perpetually in conflict. There are three basic principles I was taught to live by – good thought, good words and good deeds. These are taken very seriously by Zoroastrians. In Mumbai I visited the fire temple every day – this is an essential ritual. There was no idol or figure there but we worshipped fire. Water and fire are agents of ritual purity. We said our prayers around fire and we used the ancient language of Avesta. Zoroastrians are very strong in their belief and have strong moral norms. They have prayer competitions and I used to win prizes in them.

How did your journey out of Zoroastriaism begin?

Well, though I visited the fire temple every day in Mumbai and always wanted to help others (my mother was very kind to other people, and instilled a sense of helping others in my brother and myself), I had this inner sense that these "norms" were not enough. I was always curious about God, and asked questions about the ancient rituals and wanted to know more. The years rolled by and

I felt I did not get the answers I was seeking to the mysteries. I wondered about life after death and even had a dream at the age of seven of a light-filled place with a throne which made a deep impression on me. I just kept wondering and looked around at other people and was listening to what they said.

As a young girl in India I knew some Catholics, but they did not seem to have the sense of an "evil spirit" that we Zoroastrians have and did not seem too observant about their faith, except for going to Mass on Sundays. I asked them about what they did in church and they told me about eating bread and drinking wine and said "It's the Body of Christ", but could not explain much more to me. I asked myself, "If Christ was the son of God, why didn't God help him, take him down from the Cross? Why did God not perform a miracle and do this?" But no-one could answer my question. Now I understand better why it happened that way.

Then I had a series of tragic experiences in my life. I was married in a Zoroastrian ceremony and came to Australia with my husband but there were so many difficulties that the whole situation broke up. I was left with enormous debts from this and had to pay off about $60,000 worth of debts from a failed business venture which were not my debts in reality, but those of my husband, but I paid them off in any case. This was part of my mother's training – to do what needs to be done. Though my former "husband" apologised to me later saying "Sorry for what I have done" in leaving me to pay the debt, I just took on the burden and carried it. I think that somehow, my mother, in teaching me to "do what was necessary" for another, had some "pre-concepts" of Christianity when I think about it in retrospect. In any case, my mother died when I was 16, and my father when I was 22. And now, suddenly, I found myself alone in Australia. To put it mildly it was a difficult time for me. I used to sit and smoke (I have given it up since) and wonder "Why was I born? Where are you God? Are you alive? Will I die soon?'

and so on. I just sat and thought about these things for hours on end.

Then one day in 2002, I went for a walk in Malabar, (a suburb in south-eastern Sydney) intending to reach Malabar Beach, not far from where I was living at the time. I walked past St Andrew's Catholic church on the way, and somehow I felt that I should go in. I don't know how to explain this, but I felt the church was calling me. It was a weekday and I thought the church might be closed. I found out later, it usually is closed during the day. But at that time, on this day, the door was open. It was about July and with some trepidation, I went in, and I know this is hard to express, but I truly felt something so real, a presence, the presence of God. But I could not understand it and I thought it was all so "abnormal" and so, after being in the church for a little while, I ran away.

The next day, I came back again around the same time. Again, as I know in retrospect, the door was open when it normally should have been closed. I walked inside and again I ran home. The third time when I came back at the same time, and again it was open, I could not stop the tears. They just poured down my face and I asked myself "Why am I crying?" I stayed and cried for a long time.

What happened then?

I knew some people in the area who were Catholics because I was living and renting a place there at the time. I asked one Catholic lady if I could go to a Sunday Mass with her and so I went with her and some others to Mass. So in that way I kept coming back to this same church. Then several questions started to get the better of me and I kept asking these people: Why do you stand, why do you sit, what is the meaning of the bread and wine. I said to myself, "You have to find out." I listened to the sermons of Father Pat Hurley, I always liked listening to his sermons about the faith. [Fr Hurley since has been transferred to a parish in Sydney's south-west, Ed.]. I asked my friends many questions about the faith but, again, there were too many questions about baptism, salvation, and all and I could not get the answers I sought. At that time, I thought I would go and try other Christian groups too, in my search for the truth. I went to the Baptists and the Salvation Army and I observed them and asked them questions. It is strange for a Catholic to appreciate this, but I did not sense there was any great difference among Christians at that stage of my life. I attended Derek Prince's prayer meetings in Blacktown for two years and listened to his talks. He spoke with fire and passion and I thought "wow" but I still had the sense of not getting to the core of truth as I wanted to understand it, even though I derived much spiritual solace from these meetings. Somewhere around this time, I was given a New Testament and would read it, then fall asleep with a lot of questions on my mind. I would awake at 3 or 4 am still thinking of the problem and would edge closer to some kind of answer. Once I was asked by a friend "What is important, faith or wisdom?" and I fell asleep pondering this question, agonising about it, you could say. I prayed, as I often did, calling out "God please answer me" and when I woke up, the thought came to me that "You have to have faith. When you have faith you have wisdom." I would kneel and pray for hours. But I was going to many different Christian churches, listening to what they all had to say and was caught in a continual path of searching.

At some stage I became ill and did not know why I felt unwell. I remember meeting up with a "healing priest" from Sri Lanka, who some friends had told me about. I was in the room praying with him and he said to me at some point that I had some cancer cells in the uterus and I was blown over as I went to have a check-up and he was right. The medical report said I had "epithelia cells", that is, cancer cells at an early stage of development. I was shocked but even more so, when this priest actually prayed over me, and on further tests, the cells had disappeared. I realised I had been cured and was profoundly moved and aware of the power of God. At that stage I got to know something of Our Lady too and had attended a rosary group in Malabar, which I liked. Then I heard about the Pilgrim Statue of Our lady of Fatima and I attended the events surrounding that. I prayed the rosary a lot during the day and in the night, even while lying on my bed. This sounds strange, but at some stage I felt some kind of "evil" (perhaps demons?) as I prayed. Again I wondered why would I get this sense of evil as I prayed, and the answer came to me that I was being cleansed of evil and the cleaner my heart became, the more graces I would receive.

So in the midst of all this, did you think of conversion?

Now I know this sounds strange too but in 2006, even though I was praying the Catholic prayers of the rosary, I would still think about the Salvation Army as well, as I had been very impressed by some of their people and their good works. But again, strange to say, the thought returned to me that "I am a Zoroastrian." You see, you are born into Zoroastrianism, and it is not just a matter of habit and culture, it is a really deep thing: you live this belief and are expected to die in it. Somehow after all that I had experienced with Christians, I felt it was difficult to "let go" of the tradition and faith of my ancestors. I was interested in Christianity, I loved the prayers, I had had extraordinary experiences, but when the actual moment of "letting go" of the past came, there was a real struggle. I somehow thought I could continue with all the various groups and religious searching without facing the ultimate point of conversion. About this time, I had a dream, when I was visiting some friends in Brisbane. I remember it: I saw an enormous light and heard someone asked me, "Why are you so stubborn. Why don't you get baptised?" In the dream I answered: "But I am a Zoroastrian." Then

I sensed that the voice was Jesus and it was as if he were following me and I saw droplets of white light falling all around me. I was frightened and said in the dream, "Please don't baptise me", but I heard the voice beckoning me, drawing me into the white droplets saying, "You are one of us."

Can you imagine such a dream? I can tell you it is not easy to deal with all this. I woke up with a start and said, "Thank goodness it was a dream." However, the thought prompted by the dream continued when I was awake and I found myself speaking to and asking Jesus, "But why do you want me to be baptised?", and the answer came to me, "Because I want you to do my work" and I found myself saying something like "OK, I want to do your work."

From that time, I had the sense that Jesus was always walking with me, whether I went to a church or a club. On another occasion, I had the idea that I would go to a Mass and go to Holy Communion but then I realised that was just an ego trip on my part, for I thought I could do this without being baptised – just go and that was all. At that time as I was thinking these things, I closed my eyes in prayer and was prompted to think of the Crucifixion and Our Lady standing there and realised that Jesus on the Cross and Mary were pointing me to think of the Eucharist in a very different way. With the crucifixion in my mind I heard an internal reply from Jesus: "Look at me, this is what the Eucharist is, it is not just a piece of bread – this is why you have to be baptised." This was a very important realisation for me and I felt as if I had reached some turning point. I had realised that the Crucifixion of Jesus and the Eucharist were deeply linked and I found myself thinking, "I promise I'll get baptised." I knew then that God wanted me to be baptised.

At the same time, I spoke to some Catholic people but they seemed to take it easy about my need to be baptised. Then I searched for some other Catholic friends and ended up in a course for people intending to become Catholics. I went to confession weekly and this was a challenge to remember and confess my individual faults. After hearing a priest talk about smoking, I gave it up and have never smoked since. I learned the beauty of confession, of prayers and Catholic beliefs. I was baptised at St Christopher's in Bankstown in April 2007 and was on fire with love of Jesus in the Eucharist and with prayer. When October came, the month of the rosary, I would say the rosary as often as I could. Sometimes I prayed it at night and would not finish till 4 or 5 in the morning. I learned to pray while working and came to learn that November was the month of the Holy Souls and learned to pray for them. When I moved back to the eastern suburbs, I enrolled for the Bible study course at Randwick Sacred Heart church run by Father Tony O'Brien and Father Rate (MSC priests). I found it very good. I go to Mass at Daceyville and Father Jerzy Chrzczonowicz has helped me a great deal.

One problem at that time, however, was that I was too scared to let my brother, who was living in Canada, know about my conversion. You know, Zoroastrians would be really shocked to think that one of them became a Catholic. It made me shake to think about it. But I asked the Lord to take care of this problem for me. So what happened was strange. One day I joined a procession in the city – for Our Lady I think – and an American Catholic struck up a conversation with me. Well I told him my story and – as you can imagine – it is not every day someone hears about a Zoroastrian converting to Catholicism. He was stunned and asked me if he could write about me somewhere. I agreed and he wrote up a short account of our meeting on the internet. Then – and I don't know how this happened – my brother came to read about it on the net. Can you imagine – of all the billions of links on the net, he somehow finds that one. He rang me shocked and asked, "What have you done?" By that stage I realised that I did not have to tell him I had converted – God had taken that hard part away from me – I just had to tell him how happy I was and what it meant to me. In the end he calmed down. That is when I thought that perhaps in the future he might convert also. I am working on it.

How has conversion to Catholicism changed your life?

My life has changed 180 degrees. I feel I am now with the living God and I walk with Him, I talk with Him. I think He is rectifying me, straightening me out, putting me on the right track. Regular confession keeps me on track and the sacraments, especially the Eucharist. I asked God to let me serve my purgatory on earth and I pray a lot for the Holy Souls. I did a short course on the Eucharist and I loved it. I love the Eucharist and getting to know about it – everything about the Eucharist renews me more and more. I read the Bible every night and I am going to read about Saint Augustine because I have heard that his writings are very good. I have been told about other books to read too. It has been a long road and I am still on this wonderful journey with the Living God. .

4

A Catholic, what's that?

Fr Emmanuel Seo was born into a Buddhist family who were dutiful in following their beliefs. The following pages tell the story of how he found himself – at first very reluctantly – in a Catholic church and on the way to Christ. His journey from Buddhism to Catholicism was the greatest surprise of his life and he recounts, simply and eloquently, the thoughts, events and reflections that accompanied him on his spiritual voyage in the interview below (which took place on 13 February 2015 with myself at Holy Family Presbytery, Maroubra, where Fr Emmanuel was an assistant parish priest). He is now Master of Ceremonies at St Mary's Cathedral. The interviewer questions are in bold italics below.

Can you tell us a little of your background: where you were born, where you grew up?
I was born in South Korea in a town called Suwon in the late 1970s [Suwon is about one hour south of the capital Seoul]. I had five older sisters and I was the last child, the only son – so as a family we were eight in all. I remember my parents discussing whether they would have another child after having five girls. In keeping with their culture they wanted a boy as well as the girls. They thought they'd accept their five lovely daughters but during a discussion my mother made the comment, "No difference between five and six children." So that was a bit of background as to how I was born – I owe it to her! I was the sixth and I was a boy. My father was a carpenter and builder who was away a lot in the early

years of my life – for example, he had to go to Vietnam and other countries because of certain building contracts. From five years of age I remember seeing him at home more often.

My parents were Buddhists and I remember there was a statue of Buddha in our house – permanently encased in glass. I thought of Buddha as in some sense a deity – a good deity – so when I was frightened or down, I could turn to Buddha and feel better. We would go to the temple a few times a year and I remember we bowed a lot to Buddha. I noted the silence of the temples and one of my earliest memories is of bowing over and over again to Buddha at a ceremony. There was this sense of needing to detach from earthly realities and doing things for the sake of others. The two big days for us, as for most Buddhists, were the Lunar New Year and Harvest Day (also known as the Moon Festival in other cultures). On these days, the family would also offer food to the ancestors at the home of the first son. We believed the spirit of the person came down to be with us and even if they did not eat the food, they knew they were remembered and we honoured them.

What kind of thoughts did you have of Christians – if any?
I was aware of other religions and thought that everyone's got their god. Except that in South Korea there were some very fervent factions of Protestant Christians who were quite confrontational in their efforts to convert. I remember once, at four years of age, some Protestant evangelisers knocked on the door and, as our parents were out, and I was at home with my older sisters, out of politeness we let them in. As a boy I held a reputation for being particularly respectful towards adults. But for some reason, on this occasion when the missionaries asked if I had heard of Jesus, I remember being uncharacteristically antagonistic. Soon after they left, but an odd feeling remained, as I recognised the strangeness of my behaviour.

Had you ever heard of Catholics?
No, I just thought that Christians were one group. It was ironic that all of the children in my family were born in Saint Vincent's Hospital in Suwon. So, to that extent I was aware that it was a Christian hospital but not specifically Catholic, as I didn't know the distinction. But eventually, it was in connection with another Catholic hospital that a strange event entered our lives. One day when I was about 10 years old, my father was jay walking across the road and got hit by a taxi. While the accident wasn't too severe, he nevertheless ended up in a public hospital. Thankfully he only sustained some minor injuries, but the real issues were the sudden and unexpected complications with his chronic diabetes. One of these symptoms was the swelling of his legs, which they couldn't quite control. Eventually, he had to be moved to a bigger hospital, which happened to be called St Mary's. Not long after he entered this hospital all his symptoms disappeared – just like that – without any evident explanation. My parents were understandably astonished and discussed the meaning of this cure as they recognised it to be more than just coincidence.

They must have been thinking about Catholicism then and must have been looking into it. My parents had always said to us that a family should be united in faith and not adhere to different faiths. I distinctly remember one day when I returned home from my Year 5 class at school that my sister said to me, "Guess what. We are going to be Catholic," and she made the Sign of the Cross. I asked her, "A Catholic, what's that?" She then replied, "They're Christians." My jaws dropped as I thought of the confrontational Christian missionaries and all the antagonism we had shown them over the years. More than anything, I was confused. Then my confusion turned into deep distress when I realised we would have to go to Mass every Sunday. Back in those days Korean children attended school six days a week – five full weekdays and half-day Saturday.

The hours were long – roughly from 8.30 am till 5.00 pm each weekday and around 8.30 am till 12.30 pm on Saturdays. We also had lots of homework, so the only real free day I had was Sunday. It sounded like a bad dream – not only would my day off be occupied with a regular commitment, but to make matters worse, the time of the Mass coincided with the morning cartoon hours! Devastating as it was, I knew there would be no chance for rebellion. Thankfully, later on I discovered the Sunday school Mass, which meant I could still enjoy the cartoons. But more importantly, after many years, I would come to realise how a tragic incident – my father's accident – was in fact a blessing in disguise.

What happened then?

I remember attending the Children's Mass in the Cathedral in Suwon. Initially I sat confused as I didn't know what people were doing – standing up, kneeling, and sitting down. It seemed like I was the only one who did not memorise the prayers. Also at that time my zealous Protestant friend came every Sunday to get me to join his church, since I was a recent convert and supposedly didn't owe any loyalty to the Catholic Church. But even apart from my parents' wish, I personally had no desire to be jumping ship, as I regarded faith to be a serious commitment. Perhaps by then my interior life was already changing, because one day, I spent my pocket money (a highly irregular source of income, which I keenly guarded and saved, usually to buy toy robots) to purchase rosary beads. Somehow I had a great desire to learn the prayers of the rosary, which I learned from a Catechism book. I remembered too that Jesus had told us to go into a room, close the door and to pray to the Father, who is unseen (Mt. 6:6). So I used to go to the most private place in the house – the boiler room – to sit alone and pray.

Then another shock happened in my life. One day my parents announced that we were moving to Australia. As usual, the information was passed down to me through my sisters. Given the identity of our future residence, I then asked the stereotypical question, "Is it Austria?" Without even knowing where it exactly was, I was simply devastated and worried that we were going to migrate. Upon hearing the news, our parish priest also became worried as he thought we were too young in our Catholic faith and so might be more vulnerable to the influences of other religions. Hence he suggested that we become baptised before we left and that is what happened. We all had catechesis from a Sister Magdalene, and I remember sleeping in some of the classes as they were at night, after a long day at school. After many sessions of this catechesis we were baptised as a family. A lot of thought went into choosing our baptismal names – my sisters had the names of saints, Cecilia, Catherine, Elizabeth, Clara and Susannah. Where I was concerned, at first the idea of "Andrew Kim Tae-gon" came up – he was the first Korean to be ordained a priest, and was also a martyr. But then my father thought my full name might become too long, especially since we were moving overseas. So Sr Magdalene came up with the following solution. She said to my father, "Well, since he is your only son, and you happen to be a carpenter, you can be Joseph, your wife can be Mary and we'll call your son Emmanuel – God with us." And that's how I got to be called Emmanuel. I think she may have also mentioned something about a "feast day" (at the time I had no concept of such) occurring on my birthday. Years later, I discovered this to be the feast of the Presentation of our Lord in the Temple, which was quite appropriate. I remember the day of my baptism, my head tilting, with water being poured over me, and the sense that there were great mysteries in this, which I did not as yet understand but hoped to one day. Not long after this we made our first Confession and first Holy Communion.

Was it difficult to think of God as an absolute deity and of the Trinity after being Buddhist? And how did you view the Eucharist?

I had already imagined Buddha to be some sort of deity, but this was rather an infantile conviction without much rational reflection. I knew there was a spiritual world and I had a sense of there being a god who knew everything and could do everything. I just switched to realising that God, as the Christians understood Him, was the fulfilment of my inner spiritual desire to identify this absolute deity. That which used to be a juvenile and vague concept of deity had now become real and concrete. This was God whom I had always been aware of. And as nothing is impossible to God, I understood that He is one God in Three Persons, and I had no problem believing that the Eucharist is truly Christ's body as revealed in the Bible.

How did you settle in, in Australia?

When we moved to Australia (not Austria!) we first lived in western Sydney and became connected with the Korean Catholic community in Silverwater. It used to be the parish of Saint Stanislaus, but eventually the 103 Korean martyrs were added as co-patrons. [The Korean martyrs were the victims of religious persecution against Catholic Christians during the 19th century in Korea. The beatification of the first 103 martyrs in the 1970s by Pope John Paul II brought a surge in Catholicism in South Korea, where growth has been steady ever since].

As things turned out we ended up moving from western Sydney to Eastlakes and after attending a primary school out west, I attended Sydney Tech High School in Bexley. One of the most significant memories I have of that time is that of my Confirmation. For many weeks we endured hours of catechesis and preparation inside a small and hot church. It was during this time when I became conscious of being drawn into some very profound mysteries. Often I would pray the rosary and at times I would even be moved to pray all fifteen decades (we didn't as yet have the Mysteries of Light). I also became quite reflective of human mortality and what happens beyond death. I wanted my parents and sisters to make it to heaven and prayed a lot for my family. I started to ponder the fact that many high school Catholics seemed to lose their faith and I did not want this to happen to me. It was for me a question of integrity, so I thought, "Even when I grow up I'm going to keep coming to Mass."

My mother developed cancer when I was in Year 10 and died when I was about to begin my second year at uni. I remember asking God that if He were not against it, would He allow me to take her place. By then I understood that my will and God's will may not always be the same. Besides, if He had propositioned my mother, she would have chosen the same. My mother died and then two years later, my father also passed away. During my high school and university years, I always attended the Korean Catholic parish. A few years before my mother died my oldest sister had become a Sunday school teacher. She was one of the organisers for a high school camp. I attended this and became friends with some of her fellow Sunday school teachers. After my mother's funeral, one of those teachers informed me of a vacancy in the primary school division of Sunday school. He promptly began to encourage me to fill the position. "No way" was my response as Sunday was a day when, after Mass, I would meet my friends to eat out and play basketball. However, as much as I said "no way" I think something else was going on. One day, when I was waiting for my friend at church for a usual Mass-lunch-basketball combination, a nun came up behind me, snatched me by the arm, dragged me all the way to where the Sunday school teachers were, and asked them all to welcome their new colleague. At this point I had no intention of obliging and it apparently showed on my face. But then she took me to the hall where they used to sell noodles and asked for a free bowl for the new Sunday school teacher. Well, after the free bowl of noodles (that nun knew what she was doing) I thought to myself that I'd come along for four weeks then quit. As it turned out, I kept coming for eight years.

How did your vocation to the priesthood come about?

This was an important time in my life as it was during these years the assistant priest in my community asked me if I had thought of becoming a priest. I remember being struck by this question, along with a few others who were also asked to think about the prospect. We spent a lot of time together with the priest socialising as well as discussing our potential vocation to the priesthood. In 2004, this priest, three other young men and myself went on a European pilgrimage together. It was during our stay in Medjugorje when my friend and eventual ordination classmate announced to me that he had decided to enter the seminary. I was really stunned at the certainty he had of his vocation. But as time went on, these ideas were having some effect on me too, though nothing had seemed clear as yet. Once back in Sydney, however, I kept discerning. Then on 1 March 2004, as I was sitting in a train reading a book, I put the book down and began to reflect – it was near Strathfield Station – and asked myself what would yield a greater love in my life, marriage or the priesthood, and realised that this would come from being a priest Of course there is great love in marriage, and I imagined being married and could envisage all these scenarios of my life at various stages. But I realised I was being pulled into the direction of the priesthood. So I went to tell the priest that I wanted to study for the priesthood in Korea. As I wanted to have a little taste of what seminary life might be like, I attended a vocations weekend in the Sydney archdiocesan seminary along with my friend who had earlier decided to enter. I was deeply moved by the talks and had a fruitful experience as a whole. In my meeting with the vocations director at the end of the weekend, I informed him that I had already planned to pursue my priestly vocation overseas. While he accepted it, nevertheless he said, "Come and see me before you go."

After that weekend, I made arrangements to go to Korea. As a courtesy, I went to visit the vocations director to say goodbye. He tried to encourage me to remain but I was determined to be a priest in Korea. It was another case of my wanting something and God wanting something else. However, much to my dismay, my priest at the Korean community then began to also convince me to stay. I felt quite torn as to what to do, and eventually ended up ringing up the vocations office in Sydney after the application deadline had passed for Korea. During the first six months in Homebush, I still remained somewhat unhappy and unsure about the situation. At one point, at the beginning of the mid-year holiday, I had packed all my stuff into two large bin liners, just in case I would decide to transfer to Korea. However, I don't know what happened, but I just let the holidays slip by, and then somehow just returned to Homebush. I can't really say how it happened – I just went back. It was like I just got pulled back there. Partly, it was that I realised I already had everything I was looking for. I could do as a priest in Australia as much as in Korea – this had taken some time to sink in. At Homebush seminary I had the most wonderful formative years, and was ordained a priest on 21 May 2011.

Looking back on my life there were so many things that God drew me to that were not "my will" that I cannot help but marvel at how it has all happened. From the announcement that I was to become a Catholic, the nun pulling me to give catechism classes and the idea that I become a priest in Australia – it has all been a sequence of God's will shaping my life. I took as my ordination passage Luke 22:24b, "Not my will, but Thine, be done." As a priest I ask Catholics what difference does it make to them to be Catholic – there must be a distinction, and hopefully a positive one at that. I always invite them to listen to the voice of God and to allow Him to lead them along the great spiritual journey He wishes to take them on, and to share this with others.

5

Always seeking God: a psychologist converts to Catholicism

Meredith Secombe lives in Melbourne though she originally came from New South Wales. Meredith, a clinical psychologist by profession, has also completed a PhD in Theology at the Australian Catholic University in Melbourne. In the following pages a picture of a questioning, searching soul emerges, one which will never give up no matter the risks, no matter how hard the journey. A true seeker from her earliest days, Meredith journeyed through various expressions of Protestantism to find her way to the Catholic Church. Here she writes in response to some initial questions as to why and how she converted. This is Meredith's story.

My Early Life

I can only answer questions about my conversion from the perspective that my now 60 years has given me. They have been 60 years of seeking God. By the grace of God I was born with a driven desire to "know Truth". Reflecting on the source of this desire, I could offer a psychological explanation, but ultimately I believe it was a blessed grace given to me. Certainly the pain of a profoundly introverted personality and a reflective bent that constantly wondered why I was such a misfit in the world could account for some of the drive. It seemed to me that if I could only embrace this as yet unknown Truth, then I could be strong, grounded in something that would enable me to stand in the face of life's seemingly insuperable challenges.

I was born in Kempsey, a country town in New South Wales, and baptised in the Presbyterian church there, although we lived in Smithtown, a tiny town nearby. My mother always considered herself a nonbeliever but nevertheless had, and still has, a strong awareness of a spiritual dimension to life. She has not yet had the faith to surrender to that awareness, preferring simply to stand back objectively and to marvel at the extraordinary nature of "coincidences" and such like. My 94-year-old father has a simple and beautiful faith, but only now is able to talk about it, largely in response to conversation with his three daughters, all of us committed Christians and two of us converts to Catholicism. My parents provided a Christian upbringing, typical of Protestantism in the 1950s. I was sent to Methodist Sunday school for many years but none of it spoke to the questing depths within. There was one profound moment of spiritual infusion in my mid-teens at a Christian camp, but in the absence of much needed church support when I returned home this spiritual inflow waned.

The pain continued. I had found as a young child that the only place of relief was to move deep within and to find there a still, deep pool of quiet. As I moved into my teens, however, I increasingly felt a misfit. With an intellectual bent and a questing spirit, no-one could answer my questions. I asked what I now realise to be existential questions of both my religious studies teachers and my friends. The former provided no answers; the latter groaned in frustration.

One day a sentence came into my mind and stayed there: "Everything will stop at 30." It was to be the first of a number of such sentences that have occurred in my life, sentences which I now interpret as prophetic words from God, mindful that the scriptural condition for prophecy is that it comes true (Deut 18:22). It had the characteristic that both St Teresa of Avila and Evelyn Underhill describe as typifying God's words: no matter how many years passed, the word remained. Typically, too, the word was mysterious. I knew it meant that at 30 years of age I would be delivered from the pain I was currently in. But *how* would I be delivered? At the time, I envisaged the deliverance arriving through marriage, but when I married at nearly 24 years of age, I realised that, no, this was not its meaning. As the prophetic word indicated, I would have to wait until I was 30 to discover that meaning. The deliverance would come through another word from God, but this time mediated through a Cistercian monk. It would be the word, "You ought to become a Catholic!" But I move ahead of myself.

University Studies and Adult Conversion

I thought that perhaps university studies might lead me to the Truth that I sought. I started a BA (Hons) degree at the University of New England, Armidale, NSW, in 1970 and completed it in 1973. I had hoped, in choosing to do an Arts rather than a Science degree, that my search might be assisted. However, while philosophy, psychology and extra-curricular investigation into Eastern religions all contributed to an intellectual eclectic syncretism, they did not yield the satisfaction for which my heart yearned. My search continued.

Then, in 1973, I met some charismatic Christians at the university college in which I was living. Amazingly, they spoke in something they called "tongues"! So there was, after all, a dimension to Christianity that was not pure "head stuff", as much of my early experience of the Christian tradition had seemed to be! There was, after all, a mysterious dimension to Christianity. I did not, after all, have to go to the Eastern traditions to find mystery!

The contact with charismatic Christians opened new doors of understanding. This greatly interested me. But how was I to find the faith to believe what they believed? I prayed, "God, if you exist, please give me the faith to believe in you." My prayer was answered. After some months, I came to see that no-one other than Jesus had said, "I am the Way and the Truth and the Life." Buddha did not say this; Mohammed did not say this; Confucius did not say this; Lao Tzu did not say this. Only Jesus proclaimed that Truth was to be found in Him. At last I could believe. My friends prayed over me and I was baptised in the Holy Spirit. My joy was boundless. The sky was bluer; the grass was greener. I had found Truth! However, this was but the beginning of my journey into Christendom. I had yet to find a community with whom I could worship.

Move to Melbourne and marriage

In 1974 I moved to Melbourne, having accepted a tutorship in Psychology at Melbourne University and having been accepted into a Masters of Arts programme in psychology by research. However, at the end of 1974 I realised I was not cut out for pure academia. With regret, I converted to an applied MA in Clinical Psychology. The regret was because I had thought a pure academic research degree would help me answer the two existential questions which I had formulated in my final years at high school. They were articulated in the solipsistic, exclusive language typical of the time: "What is the nature of man. What is the nature of God?"

In response to my regret, another sentence was infused into my mind, "One day you will be able to study Truth." Blessedly, that word came true when, in my mid-40s, I embarked on what was to become 15 years of theological study at the Melbourne College of Divinity and the Australian Catholic University (Melbourne). In Hans Urs von Balthasar and, in particular, in Bernard Lonergan I found what I considered to be a complementary articulation of Truth that was utterly appealing and totally fulfilling. At last my faith was achieving understanding.

A major dimension of my move to Melbourne comprised meeting my future husband. Knowing nobody when I arrived in Melbourne, I used a *This Week in Melbourne* brochure to find a charismatic Protestant church. It was here that I met Dave as he handed out hymn books in the church foyer. Together we found ourselves on a spiritual journey for our church split, as is the tendency of many charismatic Protestant churches. We moved to a Baptist church where I received an adult baptism and it was in the Baptist church that we married. However, as time progressed our hearts yearned for more dynamic spiritual food and once again we moved, this time to a Pentecostal church some distance from home and then later to a Pentecostal church closer to home.

In these churches, there was much that was fulfilling at a spiritual level. Our hearts drank deeply from the biblical teaching and our spirits soared with the worship that was possible there. Dave played the flute and one of the pastors' wives was a trained singer who could have had a career in opera but chose instead to serve God. Both were spiritually sensitive and enabled the congregation to rise to spiritual heights of glorious worship of our Lord.

Conversion to Catholicism

Nevertheless, there was much that caused significant disquiet at a theological level. Perhaps the fact that Dave had bought, unbeknownst to the pastoral authorities, a Jerusalem Bible best expressed our silent rejection of some of the teaching. But even more significantly for me was the fact that the prayer and worship was never deep enough to touch a place within that yearned for more. Certainly, the worship took us to moments of silence wherein we felt God almost tangibly near to us. But they were merely moments, whereas I wanted to stay in that silence, to stay and to be still. The worshipping life of the Pentecostal church could not adequately mirror the deep place within my spirit that sought rest In response to my yearning, I received another word, "That which is within will be seen without." Only when I became a Catholic did I understand its meaning. To my great joy and relief I *knew* that Christ "within" was mirrored by the Blessed Sacrament "without". I could finally rest; I had found my spiritual home.

In the meantime, seeking something deeper, I spoke to older people within the Pentecostal congregation, people known for their prayer life and teaching about prayer. They could not help me; they could not speak to me of the riches of the contemplative life for which I was unknowingly searching. I prayed that God would show me the way to greater intimacy with him. Eventually, I met a woman who told me of Catholic book shops in Melbourne.

I discovered St John of the Cross who taught me how to meet my heart's desire for prayer and silence. St John taught me that faith is a "silvered-over" crystal and I embraced "dark faith" with joy and familiarity. From St Thérèse of Lisieux I learned that my hidden, contemplative life had value even though so many voices, both internal and external, called me to leave my role as housewife and mother to work professionally as a psychologist. Apropos of my concerns about preferring to be a "contemplative in suburbia" to that of a professional in the marketplace, St John of the Cross reassured me that "actives" will always criticise contemplatives.

I found, even in the context of my hidden, homely life, that the contemplative tradition was not merely a source of spiritual consolation (*and* desolation!); it was also a classroom for practical living. St Teresa of Avila, for example, taught me that it is possible both to attend to the depths of one's interiority while also attending to the demands of the world. It was, in other words, possible to listen to the "still, small voice of God" within, while at the same time engage with concerns without. St Ignatius of Loyola referred to this dynamic as "discernment" and I practised discerning God's will in the nitty-gritty demands of daily living. I wondered if this was how Jesus always did what he saw the Father doing (Jn 5:19). The riches of the Catholic contemplative tradition had been opened to me and ever since I have drunk deeply from the stream.

I was also referred to a Cistercian monk at Tarrawarra Abbey outside Melbourne. I went to him in November 1981 and asked simply that he show me how to know God better. Perplexed, he wondered what to say to me. Eventually, while qualifying his comments with the observation that it was not proper to say such a thing to a Protestant, he said, "You ought to become a Catholic." I gripped the chair, shaken to the core, with my heart totally rejoicing and my head in uproar, thinking about the sure impact on my Protestant husband. Immediately, the image of the rich young ruler came to me and I knew that I must become a Catholic even if it cost me my marriage. For a month afterwards I thought it might, but the graces gained from my meeting with the monk and my profound awareness of God's presence with me were a wonderful, encompassing support throughout this time.

The monk also said that the Lord wanted to reveal to me the mystery of Mary. As he spoke of her abandonment to God, it seemed to me that in some ways I had known her all my life. Moreover, even in my Protestant Pentecostal context, God had been speaking to me of Mary, of how she was a template for who we were to be in our utterly faith-filled engagement with and surrender to the Trinity. Just as Mary surrendered to the power of the Holy Spirit and brought forth Christ as the fruit of that surrender, so, I realised, we too are called to bring forth Christ as the fruit of our prayerful, faith-filled surrender to God. I wondered what particular, incarnated expression of Christ God would want to bring forth through me.

I could of course speak nothing of this to significant others around me. My pastor thought I was deceived by the devil and my husband was indeed shocked by my whole-hearted intention to become a Catholic. Perhaps in view of their reactions, the Lord made it clear to me that while I had embraced Catholicism in my heart, it was not yet time to embrace it publicly. I must wait. So I became a "closet Catholic", popping into Catholic churches, taking the Eucharist "by intention", loving Marian chapels, delighting in the sacramental of Holy Water, from which I never failed to receive a blessing. It was to be ten years before circumstances eventually made it possible to convert to Catholicism. By that time a friend who had been a pastor in our Pentecostal Church had joined me and so, in July 1991, we were both received into the Catholic Church, with our husbands and children watching on. It was a blessed, blessed time of great peace and joy.

Believing that husband and wife should worship together, for five years Dave faithfully came with me to Mass. Knowing Catholic teaching, he refrained from taking the Eucharist. Eventually, the Spirit of the Mass wooed him and he too became a Catholic. While he still has many questions, he has found his spiritual home and enjoys contributing in various ways to the life of the Church.

Becoming a Catholic was a great source of interior joy. Socially, however, I was at a loss. I had lost the spiritual community with whom I had identified for so many years. My husband and I had been active leaders in the church, running weekly house church meetings, counselling and supporting many people. Suddenly all of this stopped. I was still at home with school-aged children; I had not returned to work. It was a lonely time. Even the lifelong awareness of a call to an "I know not what" seemed to have left me. I could only wait.

Ever since high school I had yearned to study theology. Eventually I realised that this was now a possibility. I had completed one unit of a Bachelor of Theology in 1984, wanting to ensure that my private studies of classical spirituality meshed with 20th century

Church teachings. In 1995 I decided to resume those studies. It was a time of great joy as I enrolled at Yarra Theological Union, in the grounds of a Franciscan Monastery. I decided to study part-time, doing one unit each semester, so that gradually I could be integrated into the wider Catholic community and within which I began to make beautiful friends.

Calls to further faith

Yet something was missing. I was aware that while I truly felt I had come home in becoming a Catholic, there was yet something further to do, something more specific than simply studying theology and attending Mass. I wished to belong to a specific outworking of Catholic faith. I thought that would be found by joining the Secular Carmelites. However, a profound experience in January 1999 made it quite clear that this was not where God wished me to be. There followed yet another "desert" time, a time of waiting in dark faith and patient unknowing. Throughout the first half of 1999 a friend helped me discern the next step: God was calling me back into psychological practice.

The thought horrified me. I had grown attached to my homely contemplative life. Yet I knew that I must surrender that life, for those who save their lives shall lose them. So in July 1999 I re-registered as a psychologist and started a private practice, advertising in retreat houses throughout the Melbourne area, and offering a service explicitly to those who wished to integrate spirituality into their psychological work. I joined the Australian Psychological Society's Christianity and Psychology Interest Group and worked as a member of the committee for four years. Then I realised that God was calling me to be the convenor through yet another of those prophetic sentences that would pop into my head. Restless one night during a conference, I asked God what was going on.

The response was clear: "I want you to be convenor." For one who sought hiddenness having been a committee member was enough, but convenor, with the associated demands of running conferences and such like ...! I was deeply troubled by this new call. Yet by that time I had become accustomed to God's voice and knew that I could not refuse.

While I dearly loved those whom I served in the psychological community, colleagues and clients, the label of "psychologist" did not sit comfortably with me. It seemed to me to be an interim work, while I waited for the "real" work that God had in store for me. I wondered if my theology studies might lead me to that work. By this time I had completed a Master of Theology and had begun a Doctor of Philosophy degree with the topic, "Hearing the Call of God." This, after all, had been my lifelong endeavour and I was interested in articulating the philosophical, theological and psychological dynamics that enable such hearing.

Then, in February 2008, during prayer before the Exposition of the Blessed Sacrament, I heard "Disband your practice and surrender to love." It was a new call to step out in faith. After much discernment, I closed my practice in November of 2008, ostensibly to work full-time on my theology doctorate. A new, totally unanticipated, life was beginning, a life which called for constant abandonment and faith and trust in God, a life of challenges that I could never have envisaged, but filled with the love and joy and peace that only God can bring. Whereas the first half of my life had been the search for Christ, the wisdom of God, this second half was to be the discovery of Christ, the power of God (1 Cor 1:24). But all this is another story.

6

Something just out of earshot

Robert Tilley grew up in Gosford, north of Sydney, and for many years searched for the meaning of what he saw around him. The journey took him to many surprising places and detours, including public protest against the Papacy – but in the end, it took him to the Catholic Church. Robert is now a lecturer at the Catholic Institute of Sydney and author of several books on religious themes. He tells his story here.

If there is one feeling that I think has accompanied me through life it is that of puzzlement, so much so that when I look back to see the patterns that form the warp and woof of my life then what I see are the lines of a journey that run as a puzzle but, nevertheless, come together to form an answer. And I mean by "answer" not the kind of thing one finds at the end of a book written upside down, or an answer that having been ticked is tallied up and forgotten; but when I say "answer" I mean a response to someone who has called you. For the overwhelming sense I have had for a good part of my life, and this, I can assure you, is not simply a case of projecting back what I feel now, is as if someone has been calling my name, saying something, but what is being said is just out of earshot. And, because of this I have always had a sense of something else, something beyond, something just out of sight and out of hearing. It is this that has caused me to be puzzled by things, including everyday things, well *especially* everyday things. It's a bit like being at home and yet feeling that home is somewhere else again.

I was born in 1958 in what was once an old Roman outpost on the border of Wales and England, Chester, which was fitting for like Chester I am half Welsh and half English, for my mother, Gwyneth, was Welsh and my father, Derek, was English. Though it might be said that my father was himself something of a border-nature, for although his father's family came from Somerset his mother was of an altogether different lineage. His mother had classic Eastern European Jewish features, which given her family was no surprise for although my father would never talk about it all indicators were that his mother *was* Jewish. Her parents and family came out en bloc from the Ukraine in the early 20th century when there were mass movements of Jews from that land due to especially violent pogroms. The fact that my father would never address the subject is, I think, no surprise given the events of the War, for who could tell when another pogrom or another Holocaust might arise? It meant, of course, that my father was Jewish, something that would not have sat well with old Somerset stock. As a consequence, he was I think always trying to fit in by being the very English Man, but he overdid it and came off looking first like Terry Thomas and then, at the end of his life, like Arthur Daley (something he was rather pleased with). My father was a doctor and my mother an artist who by the end of her life had made quite a name for herself and sold in galleries across Australia. Both are long dead for longevity has not been a mark of our line. Ours was not a particularly religious family, in fact I was not baptised when little and I and my three siblings were rarely, if ever, taken to church. My mother was nominally Methodist and my father, again very nominally, Church of England. My mother taught us to pray the Our Father, but I think that was about it – but near the end of their lives they both expressed a more lively Christian faith.

One of the afflictions of childhood is boredom, and in the absence of virtual stimulation children are thrown upon their immediate environment in a way that demands they explore and make the most of what is on offer. In the houses in which we lived we had many, many books, and because of this it always meant that there were always present solid signs that spoke of other worlds; of knowledge one could only guess at. The older and dustier a book was, the more it hinted at deeper more intriguing secrets. Many of these books were inherited down through the family, and many of them came down from my mother's aunt, long deceased, I later realised that many of these books were Anglo-Catholic in nature and interspersed among them were a number of books by G.K. Chesterton. When I began to think of coming over to Rome the presence of these books hinted at a spiritual communion with someone who was family, but someone whom I had never met, and yet I felt like I knew her, perhaps even that she had prayed and was *still* praying for me and the whole family.

For whatever reason, from a very early age, and I mean very early, early as two or three, I expressed an interest in matters religious, and although I cannot remember this it was something my mother remarked upon. One thing I can remember of my first years in school in London was of being fascinated by the Bible which was at the front of our classroom, how before class started I would set about reading it. All told I was curious and two things especially intrigued me, though not necessarily in this order, these being God and ghosts. Perhaps this latter interest was the result of living in a rather big and old house in London till the age of ten, a house that was haunted – something that was the opinion not only of children but adults as well, for not a few people had rather odd experiences there. Of course I terrified myself more than the ghosts did for curiosity demanded that I search out the subject. The feeling of puzzlement, the feeling that there was something to understand, overrode the feeling of terror (well at least in the day, at night, as one cowered beneath the blankets, *that* was an entirely different matter).

We came to Australia as ten-pound-poms at the end of 1968 or early '69, and ended up settling in Gosford, or to be more specific Point Clare. We went to state schools, in my case Point Clare Primary and then Henry Kendall High School, the latter being famous for being named after a poet. It was in primary school that my interest in things, let us say, supernatural increased and I began to read about subjects such as astral travel, meditation, and other like matters, only I did so primarily through the works of that old fraud Lobsang Rampa, someone who claimed to have been a Tibetan monk but who ended up being revealed as one Cyril Hoskin a plumber from Birmingham. Anyway, I began to read around these subjects and, as it was by then the early '70s, I began to be interested in things hippy and anarchistic. So it was that I began to read the books of that other fraud, Carlos Casteneda, as well as the works of Timothy Leary, Richard Albert, Jack Kerouac, and others of like nature. It was in early high school that I began to use drugs of the psychedelic variety, having my first LSD trip at the age of 15 (indeed it was on my 15th birthday). Through some close contacts I found myself beginning to hang out at what were then called the Tin Sheds at Sydney University. In Sydney in the early 1970s the Sheds were a major centre of art and political activism, of underground comics and drugs, as well as the kind of spiritual ideas that, back then, went with those things. My use of psychedelics was always informed by the notion that they would open me up to spiritual realities, realities that I pictured in the vein of surrealist art, an art movement that, as a young teenager, I had fallen in love with.

The common theme running through all of the above was one of seeking out what it was that called to me, for it was as if I thought that I could only reach for what is beyond by dabbling in the marginal and addled. And this seems to have contradicted something else I felt, which was that this call was not *only* addressed to me, rather did it have to do with the very nature of all creation for all things were called. And yet, though I could not at the time have put it like this, although this call was of nature, was something to do with the very *beingness* of nature, nevertheless I know I had a strong sense that it was something *beyond* nature. My desire for other worlds, my young taste for things surrealist, my use of psychedelics, and my interest in things supernatural (misguided though these were), all of these I think were the confused stirrings of what it is to be truly human; which is to say, that we are made to enjoy God for all eternity.

God's providence works in many unexpected ways, for in saving us from ourselves He often turns us against ourselves in order to have us see beyond our often silly conceits. At the time, of course, it is far from pleasant. So it was that I began to have what were colloquially known as "bad trips". A bad trip on LSD is a very scary thing indeed. Only that was not all, for I started to have bad trips as well on marijuana, the conclusion of this being that in spite of what I would have wanted I left the drugs behind. Grace can be uncomfortable and inconvenient and, at the time that it works its work, one can often wish that it had delayed its arrival by a year or three. Only, looking back one sees that its arrival was opportune and timely, for one of the things I saw as I grew up in Gosford is the utterly pernicious effect of dole and dope on young males. Gosford tended to be a low employment area with an easy availability of marijuana. The combination of these two factors is reflected in a sub-class of young yobs, of which I was one, that we might call the "doldrums"; one is becalmed in a Sargosso Sea of weed, and slowly one begins to rot. In sum, the bad trips were a Godsend.

Another thing that ought also to be recounted is the political side of what was going on in my life, insofar as it involved ideas of anarchy and an attendant criminality. I and a few others, all in our mid-teens began to turn to things delinquent, not the least of which was stealing cars. I was, I guess, a precocious yob for my involvement in these activities was not primarily about material gain (very little came of that), rather was criminality for me entwined with the sense of the supernatural in that I interpreted the desire for other worlds as being one that should be attended by a breaking free of the constraints of *this* world. The interesting thing is how the sense of hurting others did not register, except, that is, when my older brother commented on this, but although this made me pause I nevertheless carried on. Until, that is, I and two others were arrested.

One afternoon, having skipped school, we were caught in a stolen car, taken to Gosford Police Station, and later sent to court. We were given a year (or perhaps two years) probation, and because it was our first offence and we were juveniles, the judge said no record would be kept. If the thought of doing harm to others had not been sufficient to stop me from thievery, then falling foul of the law did. I think too, that around this time I was beginning to sense that outlaw anarchism was vacuous and self-indulgent. Indeed, today I loathe anarchism, perhaps even more than I loathe drugs, for it is, in my opinion, little more than the handmaid of pragmatic and ruthless power. Though today's anarchists make much of opposing global capital, anarchism is the natural ally of neo-liberal economics and capitalism's cultural expression, liberal progressivism. That I had a hand in promoting it is to my shame, but all I can plead is the callowness of youth and treat the foregoing paragraph as something of an act of confession and contrition.

I was 16 and my life of crime was over. This was, however, far from being the case with my pursuit of the call, and so it was that things spiritual grew all the more pronounced in my life, and did so with an even stronger accent on other-worldliness (albeit with a little less neglect as to the well-being of others). When we were arrested a police officer asked me what it was I wanted to be, to which I replied a "tramp". Yes, it sounds like a typical smart-aleck response from a too clever-by-half adolescent, but in all honesty it was true, for what I dreamed of *was* a kind of wandering journey to find what I had increasingly come to experience as an other-worldly beauty. I had gravitated to less fraudulent and more disciplined literature, such as the study of Zen koans, but one day, feeling rather bored – see how boredom can be a means of grace! – I picked up a Gideon's Bible that was in my father's waiting room and began to dip into the Gospels. Although I had begun to read the Bible back when I was very young it had fallen forgotten, but now that I again began to read the Scriptures the voice of Christ had what was, I can only say, a remarkable effect. In particular, the passage about not caring for the morrow but seeking first the Kingdom of God, *that* passage brought everything together, all I had felt about other-worldliness and being a tramp as well as the sense of something calling and the longing to know, it spoke of these things and more in a few short lines! On reflection, Jesus spoke in a way that chimed perfectly with the tone and pitch of the puzzling call. I mean by that, that on reading the words of Jesus there is often such a sense of recognition that you simply do not even consciously recognise the moment of recognition! It is so natural, as it were, that it does not call forth any comment except that what one is reading is, well, simply true. Many years later, having just become a Catholic in 1997, I was blessed with a dream of Mary and in the dream she was so beautifully natural that everything else around her seemed, by comparison, unnatural. I think this also describes the words of Jesus as recorded in the Bible, they are so natural and yet, at the same time, so *extraordinary* that they defy explanation. One needs only see how all those people who try to mimic the voice of Christ only ever end up sounding at best silly, and at worse inane. One need only compare the real Gospels with the Gnostic ones – the Gospel of Thomas for example – to see what I mean.

Shortly after picking up the Bible I met in the main street of

Gosford members of the Children of God sect, a kind of hippy-Christian group who studied the ramblings of a certain Moses David who, among other claims to fame, wrote some of the most tedious pamphlets imaginable. It was in the street that I prayed with them for Jesus to come into my heart, and whatever happened, *something* happened. As I say, God works in strange ways and from that time things began to take more and more a definite shape, in that I set out on a path that, looking back, I can only describe as a time that seems to be shaped by a battle over my soul. This was in 1975 and near the end of the year I did a road trip to Nimbin, this being a year or so after the Rainbow Festival had set up a commune at Tuntable Falls. I was still at school, but not for much longer, for, inspired by the trip to Nimbin (as well as by Jack Kerouac, Timothy Leary, and Moomin books), I dropped out. So it was that at 17 I left home and hitched around, on and off, for some years, with periods of living in Sydney.

What happened in the following years, from 17 through to my mid-20s is a mix of strange and unsettling events, many, I think, of a supernatural nature. I believe that what I experienced were the effects of an indiscriminate and ill-informed engagement with things mystical and spiritual, so ill-informed that it did not dawn on me to ask whether or not it was within my ability to properly understand the things I was reading and practising. In short, I had little if any idea of the necessity of authoritative guidance. Add to this the use of psychedelics, and I think the result was, in a manner of speaking, that I 'burnt' my soul. I dabbled with things about which I had no proper idea, knowing little of their history, and even if they were topics that were good in themselves, it was not a good thing for a young person, on his own, to cast about, uninstructed, in such waters. Indeed, it is not good for anyone of any age to do so.

These were times full of odd events and odder people, and often very disturbing dreams as well. Although it sounds terribly melodramatic, when I think back on those years the description that suggests itself is that it was a time of demons. I drew a lot in those days, I drew cartoons for magazines (my first regular strip called "Death" was in the mid to late 1970s for the magazine *Nation Review*), but I drew more serious works as well, and they serve as something of a testimony of that period. Now here's the thing: when I look back on those drawings, not only is there a clear growing dominance of Christian imagery, a good deal of that imagery is very Catholic in appearance. Yes, it might be said that I simply picked this up from the art I studied, which is to a degree true, only, following on from the Children of God experience I was reading the Bible more and more and doing so from what can only be called a more Protestant than Catholic angle. In fact, I would soon begin to draw specifically anti-Catholic pictures. Nevertheless, I look back on some of these drawings and from this side of the years they look very, very Catholic indeed.

To jump over some years, in the early 1980s through the works of a number of Protestant popular writers, I began to grow in the apprehension of God's love and His grace, and was baptised (in the Uniting Church) and then joined the Gosford Presbyterian Church where I was "confirmed" and remained a member for about eight or so years. It was here that I became an ardent Protestant of the Calvinist variety – a Reformed Presbyterian. Not that this was so much the fault of the Gosford Church, by no means, rather as I read up on Calvinism, as I studied the Westminster Confession of Faith, as I took the presuppositions of Calvinism seriously and followed out its logic, I was led to conclude that to be a faithful Protestant one ought to be a thorough Calvinist (whereas others might have said it made one into a thorough pain in the neck).

Calvinism, I would argue, is the logic of a certain view of grace taken to an arbitrary end. I mean by this that in Calvinism the accent is on predestination such that God decides before He has made anybody that He will make all so that they sin and, because of that, He decrees that they all should be tortured in hell for eternity, but that He will save some and not others. (Some Calvinists believe that the decree of predestination to hell or heaven logically preceded God's decree that humanity should sin.) In hyper-Calvinism (which is really consistent Calvinism) it is therefore held that Jesus died not for everyone, but only for the elect – this being called "limited atonement". This doctrine of what is called "Double Destination" is held to be the expression of God's grace in that plainly no one has any real efficacious role or even choice in their salvation, indeed that grace is ultimately expressive of divine arbitrariness. Certainly, in the history of Calvinism some argued that it was more a matter of fore-knowledge: God knew who would sin and who would not – but this is a quibble, for as God knew that all would sin then God still decided to save some and damn others *before* they had *actually* done anything at all.

The logic of Calvinism is that God becomes the author of both good *and* evil, worse still it makes of God to be more of a devil than the Devil, a point to which I will return. Most Presbyterians do not hold to this theology, not because they have consciously argued otherwise but more by reason of indolence and inconsistency, and although this saves them, as it were, from having to believe wicked things about God, it also, in my opinion, blinds them to the need to make a decision as to whether or not to stay within the Reformed faith or leave it. And, in not making that decision they deprive themselves of the chance to find the fullness of the Christian faith, in all its proper tensions and balances, in the Catholic Church.

But Reformed Calvinism is absolutely opposed to the Catholic Church, seeing her as the Whore of Babylon as described in Revelation. Furthermore, the Pope is an anti-Christ and the Mass an idolatrous blasphemy. (I should stress that the majority of Presbyterians do *not* hold to these notions, only the very Reformed among their number do so.) And so it was that when John Paul II came to Australia in 1986 I felt duty bound to make my feelings known, and managed to get my picture in the *Sydney Morning Herald* carrying a sign that read "The Mass is a blasphemy and the Pope an Anti-Christ" as a I demonstrated outside a Mass for youth at the Sydney Showground. What can I say? This side of having been a Catholic for 15 years I wonder if John Paul didn't see the photo in the paper and pray for me. It's also rather ironic that one of the works that confirmed for me that I should enter into the Church was his *Crossing the Threshold of Hope*.

Back in 1985 I did an Adult Entry course into Sydney University, my aim being to complete an Arts degree so that I could go to Moore College in order to train for the Presbyterian ministry. (In those days the Presbyterian Church sent their candidates for ministry to Moore College which is the college for Sydney Anglicans.) But as it happened other matters intervened, matters that led me to leave the Presbyterian Church in the early 1990s. It's difficult to say when exactly I left for it was a slow and protracted process. What led me to leave? It would, perhaps, be better to ask what was it that led me to begin to allow myself to question the precepts of Calvinism.

A number of things happened that led me to question whether or not I was of the elect, and in order to search out a resolution to this matter I allowed every doubt and objection I had to the Calvinist faith to surface. The long and short of it was that I could not accept that God could create sentient beings just so that He could damn them for eternity, and that in doing so He would derive pleasure from this and that this would redound to His glory. Nor could I accept that in believing this I was honouring the concepts of love and grace. It seemed to me that this was to so redefine the words "love" and "grace" that if true then nothing at all was sure for all of us, elect and non-elect alike; we could never be sure of anything at all. After all, if love and grace can be redefined to mean the deliberate intention to create people to torture for all eternity then what does anything mean? What does "truth" mean? If this was God then He was capable of anything, including deciding to go back on decisions He had made concerning who was or was not predestined for heaven or hell. In Calvinism, God is ultimately arbitrary and nothing certain can be known of Him, something that makes a mockery of revelation as well – might it not be that what we understand as truth is, as far as God is concerned, a lie, and that a lie is, in fact, true for Him? A will that is arbitrary can redefine anything to mean anything at all, and though one might think one is of the elect, has all the definite signs of such, exhibits all the fruits, ultimately it all means nothing for God could redefine the signs of election to be instead signs of predestination to damnation.

The long and short of it was that I left the Presbyterian Church in the early 1990s. For the next few years I did my degrees at Sydney University in Biblical Studies, Divinity and Philosophy. I also went out clubbing and partied a lot, albeit sticking only to alcohol when I did. But matters religious were always to the fore, and although I tried seriously to consider atheism I found it, as I think I always have, to lack substance and to be superficial when it came to philosophy, art, and anything requiring critical reflection. I again looked at other religious teachings and although there is much to commend them nevertheless, after a few years, I knew that I still held to three basic Christian dogmas: the Trinity; the Incarnation; and grace. I also still held to high regard for the Bible for, even though I had spent many, many years studying modern biblical criticism I found its assumptions historically tendentious and its method as arbitrary as the God of Calvinism. By way of postscript to this period and to be fair, I should acknowledge that from Calvinism and Evangelical Protestantism I learned to critically analyse the claims of modern biblical criticism. I am also of the opinion that my time in Calvinism, with its narrow basis and its narrower logic, served as a kind of healing balance to the more mystic practices that I had pursued prior to my time in that Church. It served as a rigid cast of sorts to bind some broken bones.

It was around 1993-94 that I began to think seriously as to where I should go given that I realised that I was still a Christian, and the moment that I thought of the Catholic Church the answer was obvious. Or rather, what I should say is that *the feeling* was obvious, for as with the reading of the words of Jesus so too with the consideration of the Catholic Church, it just seemed the most natural thing of all. It felt as if I not only heard what it was that had been calling to me, but that I had known what I was being called to all the time. When I think of it like this it still puzzles me, and yet the feeling that I had, a feeling that was both of the body and the soul because of the spirit, this feeling was simply "Well yes, this is it, obviously so." But although the heart said yes, nevertheless in good conscience I could not cross over to Rome for there were still doctrinal matters that I could not in, good faith, assent to. I had no real problems with the primacy of St Peter and the necessity of a visible authoritative and hierarchical Church, for now it struck me as plain that that is what the Bible teaches. But transubstantiation and the role of Mary (and the intercession of the saints) were issues for me, and I had honestly to confront them and see if I could assent to them in good conscience. The long and short of it is that I did, albeit it took two or three years of study, which studies dovetailed very nicely with the subject of my doctorate which concerned the question of how the sacred text is to be read, following the lead of St Paul's reading of the sacred text.

In the midst of all of this, that is in the mid-1990s, there were again many, I guess, supernatural events and, for want of a better term, mystic transports, but by this time I knew that they had to be subordinated to the judgement of reason and to Christian doctrine – only which Christian doctrine? And as noted above, I was coming to realise that the fullness of Christian doctrine is to be found in the Catholic Church.

Now, there was one event in particular that set me on this path, and it was the result of a whim. I was with a friend on a day out driving from Gosford to Newcastle, and on the way back to Gosford I suggested we do some exploring, so we pulled off the main road and began to drive through some suburbs till we came to a beach. It was evening and already getting dark, and on the beach I had such an experience of God's love, so overwhelming was it, that then and there I think I could have renounced the world, stripped myself of all things, and devoted myself entirely to God. The person I was with was, I think, oblivious to this, she to this day being an atheist, but from that night on I was restless, for I suppose I wanted that experience back – and alas it still hasn't come back. I can honestly say, without any equivocation, that if you were offered every imaginable sexual pleasure, the greatest drug induced high, the most expensive luxuries and delicious dishes possible, and top them all of with undreamt of wealth; if you were offered these and more, or in place of them you could have this experience of God there would be no question which you would choose – *no question at all*. You simply would not even pause to think about it, all those other things would have *no attraction at all*. I think that for an all too brief moment I was allowed to hear the voice clearly, the voice that I think has always been just out of earshot; or better still to know something of the one whose voice it is, and to know that in such a state there is no puzzlement but a wonderful sense that, well, it all makes sense, for God *is* love.

What I would later learn from partaking in the treasures of the Church's teachings and Her repository of wisdom, is that such experiences as this do not count against systematic theology and dogma, but are, in fact deepened and given their due stability and substance through that dogma. As I have said, one of the problems

I encountered while a youth was the lack of religious substance and authoritative guidance, a lack that to this day I feel endangered my soul. But here's the thing: what I learned from Calvinism is that there are systematic theologies and there are systematic theologies. The Calvinist system is a system predicated upon certain fundamental errors that work themselves out in a logic of increasing exclusion; a schismatic system whereby the so-called elect, those said to be loved by God, becomes a smaller and smaller group, until one begins to think that perhaps one is the last remaining member on earth. And then, of course, one begins to doubt even that!

By way of contrast, what began to attract me about the Catholic Church was its unity, and although to this day I am no friend of so-called liberal theology, nevertheless back in the mid-'90s I liked the fact, and still do, that the visible Church can contain groups as diverse as Liberation Theology and Opus Dei. To this day I delight in the fact that again and again I find out that the Church is far more charitable than me. It is this unity in diversity which the Catholic Church has that expresses an inclusive logic, and this inclusiveness expresses the fact that it is indeed founded upon Jesus Christ and thus upon *the fullness* of the grace of God. She is thus the natural and supernatural grounding necessary for the kinds of practices I pursued from early youth on up, and She also provides the kind of systematic theology, with all its proper tensions and balances, that can speak of mysteries such as predestination, but prevent them from becoming unbalanced heresies that make God out to be a devil. If there is one thing that I feel I can do by way of reparation for my years of opposing the Church, it is to be committed to the unity of the visible Church. For I think that if there is one thing that cradle Catholics do not properly appreciate, and this applies both to so-called liberal *and* ultra-conservative Catholics, is just how important this unity is and how easy it is to take it for granted. Having been party to, and promoted, a system of schism par excellence I have some experience of the kind of conceit it inculcates, the motto of which could be a phrase that a friend of mine coined, "I am mad, and I am right!"

I entered the Church in 1997, at St Brigid's in Marrickville, Sydney. There were two things in particular which came together that night that served as a kind of mystical confirmation if you like of the rightness of that decision. Since I had that experience on the beach I had also a growing sense of the centrality of the mystery of the Cross, of the suffering of our Lord on the Cross, and this for a number of reasons I cannot go into here. Suffice it to say that the Passion of our Lord increased as an object of contemplation and study for me. I did not plan it this way, and I only discovered it sometime later after I started the RCIA course, but St Brigid's Marrickville is run by the Passionist Fathers.

The second thing is entwined with this in that both support the other. I should stress that to this day matters liturgical are rather beyond me, and while I was a Calvinist I even thought it wrong to observe Easter and Christmas (not all Calvinists think this way). I say this because I had no idea when I started the RCIA course that I would be received into the Church on the Saturday night Easter Vigil, but I was very happy to learn that this was the case. I was especially happy when I went through my diary and realised that the night of that experience on the beach, a night many years previous, was on the Easter weekend. God, I think, gives us gifts over and above anything we might expect!

The night of my reception was a glorious night, and if you know St Brigid's you will also know that they put on a good spread for the breaking of the fast at the end of the Vigil Mass on Saturday night. It was a sumptuous celebration and one I will never forget, and one for which I feel a deep gratitude to those who made it so at St Brigid's.

Since then I have learned both of the humanity of the Church and its divine nature. In respect of its divine nature one thing in particular stands out, the Mass. Intellectually and biblically I had come to accept the doctrine of transubstantiation, but the way in which it grows on one is something rather astounding, especially given my low propensity for matters liturgical. Much the same can be said for the Rite of Reconciliation: why more Catholics do not avail themselves of the sacrament is a bit baffling. Then there are the treasures of the Church. To this day one stumbles across new forms of devotions and practices that in their variety and colour, and often unparalleled oddness, make the Church to be like a wonderful country fair.

As for the humanity of the Church – and there's a lot of it! – at times it can be a dispiriting thing, until, that is, you remember Jesus' words and take them seriously: "I came to call sinners and not the righteous." One of the problems I had as a Calvinist was the tacit idea that the Church should be more akin to a pumping gym full of able-bodied people in glowing health, than to a hospital that sets out to heal the weakness and wounds of sin. So it's no surprise, then, that in a hospital one finds sick people, and in the true Church of God one finds sinners, lots of them, lots and lots of them, which is why, I guess, one feels truly at home.

7

A Muslim becomes a Catholic

Here is the story of a Sydney ex-Muslim who became a Catholic after many trials, upheavals and anguish in her personal life, not to mention threats from certain members of her family. This story was related to me via an extended telephone interview and this is a record of that conversation. Sabah (not her real name) sounded very happy to share her conversion story – for she says that her conversion was the greatest joy of her life.

Sabah originally comes from Cairo. She has a Bachelor of Law degree from Cairo University and has business qualifications from Cairo and the University of New South Wales, Australia. She was born into a Muslim Egyptian family where her father was a judge who died young at age forty-six and her mother was a housewife. Sabah was the eldest of three children and born into a not very strict Islamic family in terms of practice.

Early in her life Sabah noticed discrimination against Christians when she was studying law at Cairo University. She had to study Sharia law and while she studied she met Christians along the way with whom she had conversations. She always thought of them as nice, peaceful, even beautiful people. She says she "could see peace in these people – they were humble – they were discriminated against, spat at and abused ... but they were still happy." Sabah said that by contrast, from the Islamic point of view, to be happy in such circumstances would be rather to show them up as cowards.

When Sabah was studying Roman history she was able to get a tutor to help her. She felt as if she did not know as much as her

Christian peers who had a greater grasp of it. Then in second year she saw clear discrimination in that the Christian students were failed in a particular subject but she was given a distinction. Knowing that this was not a fair mark she complained about it to her mother. She knew she could not do anything about it but she needed to tell someone how she felt.

At that stage she was in a receptive frame of mind to accept an invitation to come to a Christian church, where she went incognito. She was moved at the sight of Christians praying, saying "I found peace in this church as if the Holy Spirit was with me there. I cry even when I remember how it was. The people there seemed to have been abused and crucified." Every Sunday she continued to go to that church. She was also obliged to go to the mosque but her feet would go very slowly when approaching.

As time passed she met a man and married him. As it turned out he was a Muslim who was not a strict one and he even came to a Coptic Orthodox church with her. They had a daughter and decided to emigrate to Australia in the early 1970s with their young child. When in Australia, while she moved in Muslim social circles, she attended the Coptic Orthodox church in Sydenham and then recalled at some point seeing a movie called *Christ the King*. It was the beauty and goodness of Christ that overwhelmed her. She said she could not get over how "beautiful" Christ was, how he healed the sick. When he was crucified in the movie she was very emotionally affected by it. She recalled thinking, addressing Christ saying, "You came with peace, but Mohammed came with the sword." At that point she started to called Jesus "Lord" and to pray to him ... She recalls asking Jesus, "What happened to him?" (referring to Mohammed) and was unable to discern any answer.

Then she had some upheavals in her life. Her marriage broke down and she had two children to look after. She says her husband was not an honest man and she was on her own with two children with no support. She did receive some help from male and female friends and later met another man – let's call him John – and ended up marrying him. He also was a Muslim. She tried to link up with Egyptian Catholics who warned: "They will kill you" – referring to Muslims who would learn of her attraction to Christianity. When a Maronite friend took her to church the priest was very wary of her as she still was officially a Muslim.

Then some time later, Sabah found herself in Cabramatta one day and felt drawn to go into the Catholic Sacred Heart Church there. She actually met the then Father Chris Toohey and said to him, "I want to learn about Christianity."

He asked her, "Are you an atheist?"

Sabah said, "No."

He then asked, "Are you a Christian?"

She answered, "No,"

She then said to him, "I am in the darkness and I want to see the light."

Fr Toohey asked her, "What light?"

She answered, "The Lord."

Sabah says that Fr Toohey seemed somewhat surprised to learn that she was a Muslim. However twice a week he taught her about Catholicism and she said that she felt as if she were being born again. She was baptised in October 1983 and recalls the church being full because of all those attending Mass. When she walked down the aisle of the church she said she felt the Holy Spirit with her.

It was at this time everything fell apart in her second marriage as John was angry at her conversion and took the son to stay with him. Her 14-year-old daughter stayed with her but then was torn between her mother and her father. Sabah said that Muslims she met spat on her having heard of her conversion and threatened her even at work. One of them she recalls showed her a knife during an interlude at work and exclaimed: "You are a sacrifice." She was involved in a bitter property settlement in court which resulted in a great loss of money for her.

Sabah then learned that her mother in Cairo had disowned her and had had a stroke which was attributed to Sabah's conversion to Catholicism. Sabah sought advice from Fr Toohey who told her to "fear only God". She said some of the members of her family were in the Egyptian secret service and one was even a general in the army and they sent her a message, "We'll kill you." Sabah thought "If they kill me that's my blood for Jesus."

Despite these threats she wanted to go to see some relations in Egypt and had tentatively booked a ticket, but took the step of praying about it first before she confirmed the trip. She asked advice of her godmother in Australia who said, "Pray to the mother of God and if it is too dangerous she will tell you not to go." Sabah said she prayed and fasted for 15 days and then received a phone call from her brother in Egypt who said these exact words: "If you come I will kill you and drink your blood." All that Sabah could think of was, "Thank you mother Mary for letting me know how things stand." She did not confirm the ticket and did not go to Egypt, seeing this as a direct proof that Our Lady had saved her life. She has not been back to Egypt since.

She had a dream not long afterwards in which she saw someone riding a donkey – it was near Easter time. She asked, "Who are you?" and there was no answer from the person in the dream. "On Holy Thursday the same person came to me in a dream wearing light brown clothes and had bread in his hand. He told me all the apostles' names. I did not know what to make of it but Fr Toohey said this is Jesus saying, 'I'll never leave you'." She said she was asked to pray for a reunion of her immediate family and she did do so for many years.

As the years went on her prayers were answered and her children understood their mother and her journey better. They stood by her and increasingly gave her their support. Her son asked for his mother's forgiveness and spoke beautifully of her when he himself was to be married. She felt as if peace returned in that way. She lives in a small flat but is overjoyed that her children returned to her, as she says, in a "psychological and spiritual" way. One of the saddest events however that she had to live through was the death of her mother not long after her conversion. She said that she herself was given many health problems after her conversion too.

One of the strangest things to have happened to her, however, is that some of the people who wished her harm, themselves contacted her and asked her to pray for them when they were ill and had problems. Sabah was known by now as a person of deep prayer who would always agree to pray for them and had no hard feelings. She says that she lives according to God's will for her and expresses the following very Catholic thought: "When we carry the cross, the Lord helps us."

Sabah finished the interview with me with a prayer she often prays: "Lord I need you, I love you, I praise you, I serve you, I trust you. Have mercy on me. You will always be in my heart." She tells all her friends, "Thank and praise him at the end of each day, thank him for the Cross, thank him forever."

8

A Lutheran pastor's journey to Catholicism

The following story recounts the spiritual journey of Peter Holmes from Lutheran pastor to Catholic convert. It is a synthesis of an online diary which Peter wrote for his children and made available to anyone who wishes to read it. The following pages give a brief outline of some key moments of Peter's extraordinary journey. Though born in Victoria, he now lives in Sydney. He is married with eight children and currently lectures in Scripture, Theology and Biblical Languages (Hebrew and Greek) at Sydney's Notre Dame University.

"I never dreamed of becoming a Catholic" – Peter Holmes

Peter Holmes was born in the town of Traralgon in Gippsland in south-eastern Victoria, in a house situated on farmland near the small town of Gormandale. Peter spent his primary school years in that small town, and travelled to high school in Traralgon. At the age of 20 he was baptised in a Lutheran church in Box Hill, Melbourne, and later entered seminary and the Lutheran ministry.

At the beginning of his ministry as a Lutheran pastor Peter found himself saying to his friends, "I've never felt so right about anything in my life." His focus was almost exclusively on a "back to basics" approach in his teaching and preaching. He adhered closely to the Lutheran understanding of doctrines handed down by Christians for 2,000 years – baptism, Eucharist, confession, and so on. He enjoyed helping people and deepening his knowledge of the faith. The only dark cloud he found on the horizon was the issue of the ordination of women which was to be discussed and voted on at a synod of the Lutheran Church of Australia.[5]

Peter had joined with many other concerned Lutherans in planning the best possible approach to "preserve the doctrine of the church" which they understood as holding that men only could be ordained to the ministry.

At the synod, an older, well loved and respected pastor insisted that Lutherans would need to call another ecumenical council in order to have enough authority to alter the church's doctrine on ordination. Peter says that this raised the question for him, that is, how did the Lutheran Church have the authority to do anything it has done, especially formulate ministry and doctrine at the time of the Reformation. Would it be necessary to have the whole of Christendom in the gathering? Peter knew that Lutheran doctrine held that the church is both visible and invisible – invisible in not being bound to any particular structure or earthly authority but visible in that it can be "seen" wherever the Word is preached and the sacraments rightly administered. How could one gather such a church without having an authority to say who was in and who was out? Peter realised that since a mere human authority could never be trusted to complete this task alone, such an authority could only be divine.

Another argument presented at the synod stated that the onus was on the contra case to prove that Lutherans could *not* ordain women, using the analogy of infant baptism. Just as Scripture did not clearly command infant baptism, yet Lutherans baptise infants as it can be justified by inference from Scripture, or (at least) from the fact that nothing from Scripture explicitly prohibits it.

As some mustered arguments and counter proofs that Scripture did indeed command against women's ordination, Peter had to admit to himself that he baptised infants, confident it was God's will because it was the unbroken practice and teaching of the church from Christ's time until now, not solely because he happened to think it was explicitly commanded in Scripture!

When some pointed out that many women had been ordained in the church throughout the ages, he pointed out that in these cases the offending group had been declared heretics. It was at this point, that "the rubber hit the road", according to Peter. The first shock was that "when one of those I was talking to pointed out that, unless I believed the Roman Church had the authority to declare what was true and what was heresy, I could not rely on their decision on these matters." Furthermore, "it would be impossible to appeal to Rome's authority without also accepting their 'authoritative' declarations on Marian doctrines, on Purgatory, on the Saints, and so on". Unless he placed store in his own ability to interpret and discern infallibly, he had no other rock to stand on – unless there were some other solid, unchanging infallible authority. This realisation immediately preceded the vote on women's ordination at the pastors' conference and Peter recalls he "went home that night in a spin".

The second shock came when he realised that no matter how sure he was, he could never insist that his own opinion was equal to God's will, even if he claimed to base his opinion on God's Word. He says of this turmoil:

> I realised that, if I could not trust my feelings and conviction, I could hardly trust the gathering of pastors next morning. Even if they were the wisest men on the earth, they could not claim infallibility even if they acted as if they were infallible. You see, making any sort of binding declaration that concerns salvation or claims to be God's own truth, is an act that assumes infallibility. Because, if you are prepared to stake your salvation on something, it must be the surest thing one could hope in. It must be guaranteed to be true! (quotation from Peter's account

on http://veritasvosliberabit70.blogspot.com.au/ – all subsequent quotations in this chapter are taken from this site).

He began to wonder how he could be sure anything was true at all:

> So, uncertain about all things, I wept. Strangely enough, I did not feel uncertain about WHAT was true, just about my authority to insist on it as binding on Christendom. Each pastor, in debating and casting his vote, was assuming a certain authority to decide what the truth of the matter was. I could not, in good conscience, pretend that I knew without doubt the mind of God.

Peter recalls praying the entire night. After he returned to Melbourne he found himself thinking deeply about the nature of truth. Several possible answers presented themselves:

1. There is no truth; everything is relative.
2. There is truth, but we can never be sure we know it.
3. There is truth, and God has provided a means of knowing what it is.

The first answer he knew was, and is, meaningless. In philosophy, science and theology it simply does not hold water. Besides, if it is true, it would logically disprove itself!

The second answer is meaningless since it is (practically speaking) the same as the first. What is the use of absolute truth if our knowledge of it is uncertain? And how can we even assert that such truth is absolute if we can only ever know it exists by relative means? This is the main logical problem with the "Scripture alone" argument. While never doubting Scripture's infallibility, what use would an infallible Scripture be without infallible means to interpret it?

Peter concluded that for anything in life and faith to "work", to make sense, to provide surety, the third option was the only option. The other choices logically result in nihilism. Besides, what sort of God would set out to save His people and provide salvation for them, but leave them uncertain as to what path to follow to receive His gift of eternal life? This would not describe an all-loving God at all.

He turned to Lutheran responses to the question: "How do we know the truth?" The first answer Lutherans give is that we know truth through the word of God. While tradition, reason and the church have some function of guidance, the only infallible guarantee of truth is the "clear" word of Scripture. If anything about Scripture is unclear, then the reliability of any interpretation is only as good as that of the interpreter.

The problem, of course, is that some Scriptures are plainly not clearly obeyed (in their literal sense). Imagine if we all advocated stoning of adulterers? Yet that particular Scripture is clear! Peter, like his fellow Lutherans had to read all of Scripture together in order to discern its clarity, to see that "Scripture interprets Scripture." That is, the clear parts of Scripture interpret the unclear parts. But then Peter asked, "Which part of Scripture applies to which other part?" To make any such judgement is actually an act of interpretation! To interpret any text in any way that is contrary to the simplest, literal meaning is to apply and claim the authority to interpret. Something that Lutherans deny any human can claim.

Then arose the question of sola scriptura. Peter simply asked why we should base everything on sola scriptura:

> Why insist on Scripture alone? From where do we gain this principle? And on what basis do we make it the founding principle of our theology? There is no such principle in Scripture itself, nor can one be derived from Scripture by inference. So where else can we find support for this

assertion? If we seek to prove sola scriptura we can hardly go outside of the very Scriptures we are claiming to hold 'solely' to in order to prove our principle. That would contravene the very principle we are trying to prove!

And then there was the issue of which Scriptures? Peter asked why the deuterocanonical books or even the Old Testament are included in the Bible. Can anyone, like Luther, reject James' as "an epistle of straw"? He asks:

> If we go along with the modern Protestant assumption that whatever is included in a Bible we buy is genuine, we are still faced with the question: "Why do we not include the seven deuterocanonical books?"

The Church cannot create the infallible Scriptures solely by human authority, but she does recognise them by the divine authority Christ has given her. If God's word is infallible by definition, how do we know what is His word and what is not? Some Lutherans like to argue that they simply accept the books that "everyone" accepts. The problem with this, of course, is that the heretic Marcion, together with many others through the ages, had not accepted the canon. Without anyone in authority to define the canon, Peter realised there was no clear truth to be had there.

The second answer Peter received to the question as to how he knew what is true was: "We decide what is true in Synod." Upon which Peter reflected:

> I began to wonder not only if the LCA is right in claiming such authority, but is the LCA even a legitimate part of the Church? To justify the validity of any claim made by the LCA one needs to rely on that much "claimed" authority. The implication is that the authority and infallibility of any group's decisions is reliant on the infallibility of its decision making process, and of those involved in that

process. The problem is that the LCA deliberately and openly rejects any notion of its own infallibility. Yet it builds its "infallible truths" on this fallible foundation!

Peter asked himself: Does the Lutheran Church of Australia (LCA) have the authority to make such a decision?

Having realised that the synod's infallibility is questionable at best, Peter noted that there were some who simply didn't believe there is an infallible way to know truth, and so they advocated a synod as a sociological method to arrive at a decision. Synod is a decision making machine which expresses the will of the people of the LCA and nothing more. Presumably then, the LCA as a body, becomes nothing more than a co-operating body of people who confess similar things.

A fourth view concerns personal conviction: a person is convinced he/she knows truth and bases all of life on this truth. Peter says of this view, "It should be obvious by now why this answer did not impress me. Besides, as a friend once said, preaching a truth based on a personal conviction has only a legitimate audience of one. If I am deciding what is true for me, then I may only preach this truth to the one person it is true for. Me!"

Peter's dilemma grows

Peter realised that first, if there were no truth, then nothing would make sense at all – physically, mentally or spiritually. He also realised revelation would make no sense at all if it was not accessible as far as faith and morals were concerned. The very existence of nature, the end of logic, the musings of the philosophers are enough to point to the existence of an ultimate reality. The Scriptures themselves deal with this reality not only as if it exists, but as if we can know it clearly. If we suggest that reality or truth are not clearly knowable we must discount revelation, and thus

Christianity, altogether. The Scriptures, however, are not simply a collection of pious writings or spiritual reflections. The Scriptures are united in their witness to the one truth, evident in the unified witness of creation, history, logic, philosophy, and in the person of Jesus Christ. If there is no knowing the truth, there is no Christ. Thus, no salvation.

Peter understood, moreover, that if there is no way or hope of finding truth, then all is meaningless. This life (if indeed it is a life) becomes a pointless and despairing existence which cannot reasonably hope for any sure end. And if there is no hereafter, nor a greater being, and that makes our actions and lives here equally as pointless. Though Descartes seemed unsure of anything save his own existence, doubting the reliability of his own senses, he knew that the senses themselves do pass information and sensations to each person. No matter how much we may doubt the ability of our senses to relate the truth, they do relate that something to us is "knowable".

Catholics and Mary

Along this journey Peter had to face the accusation that Catholics advocate worship of Mary. Looking back Peter reflects that he is "amused at how easy it is to defend this doctrine and devotion, and how deliberately antagonistic to Catholicism one has to be to ignore the evidence". Peter came to understand:

> A. Objections to Mary being called "Mother of God" can be dismissed almost immediately since the rejection of Mary as "Mother of God" has been considered formal heresy since the great councils clearly defined the Trinity and the two natures of Christ. I should point out that Lutherans, or the Confessions at least, do consider Mary as Mother of God. Luther himself calls her Mother of God, Queen of Heaven, asking her intercession in his commentary on the Magnificat!

B. The charge of Idolatry is equally absurd. We pray only to God, but we can ask others to pray for us, and with us. In fact the Scriptures urge us to do so. Sometimes we ask those Christians we know in the flesh. Other times we might ask those who are already in heaven with God.

C. There is not enough space here to deal with the "It's not in Scripture" routine. I recommend Joyce Little's book titled *The Church and the Culture War* which changed my thinking on Mary, and on faith.

Peter had no problem with Mary.

Increasing difficulties

At this point, Peter found it increasingly difficult to carry on preaching and teaching the Lutheran doctrines in good conscience. He told his bishop of his struggle, and engaged in long conversations with senior theologians. Peter prepared the following paper at the point of his momentous decision. It is worth quoting at length as a "life testament":

> Each week I stand at the front of my congregations and say "on behalf of my Lord Jesus Christ and by his command, I forgive you". I claim to speak with the authority of Jesus Christ as I forgive the sins of those gathered there. This claim is repeated in the consecration and administration of the sacraments where I claim to be called by Christ himself into this ministry, authorised by Him to speak with the same authority as if the Words came from His own mouth. On what basis can I make this claim? Not everyone is given this authority, so how can I be sure I have it?
>
> I was taught in Seminary: "Because Christ called you through His Church, hands were laid on you, and the Church declared you one of its apostolic ministers." But I am not called to the Uniting Church, nor to the Anglican

Church, nor to the Mormons. In fact, I am only called to those people in the communion called the LCA. My call, my authorisation, came solely from the LCA. The question is; has Christ given the LCA such authority to pass on?

I could rely on my own conscience under Scripture telling me that the Lutheran Church has Christ's authority, in spite of all the opinions and arguments to the contrary. Or I could simply trust the interpretations of the senior theologians of the LCA. But, even among Lutherans in Australia, we have a wide range of opinions on key doctrines. The recent debate regarding women's ordination, for example, put on public display the huge variance of opinions on the doctrines of Church, ministry, sacraments, the Holy Spirit, and these impact significantly on all the major articles of faith. So how do I know which interpretation is right and why the rest are wrong?

While I believe that God clearly reveals his truth to us for our salvation in the Word, experience tells me that I can fall into error no matter how sincerely I seek the truth. ... So how do I know if our interpretation of Scripture which validates my ministry is truth? What if we are wrong?

... Christians from the earliest times have looked to those called, appointed and authorised by Christ to speak His Word into each new context with His own authority ... Is it possible that they are wrong, or are they somehow free from the possibility of reading the Scriptures wrongly?

It boils down to this. I stand and claim to exercise the authority of Christ each Sunday, and most days of the week by who I claim to be, and by what I claim to do ... I am no longer convinced that the LCA can claim Christ's authority to ordain, forgive, or any such thing, with any surety. So how can I, in good conscience, stand in my congregation THIS SUNDAY to speak and act as if these claims were true?[6]

After presenting this paper at a meeting of pastors, Peter realised that those present could not answer his questions and that the day of his resignation was drawing ever closer.

Resignation

One can only imagine the anguish Peter lived through. He knew that, if he was convinced that the Lutherans were unable to answer his questions, he would have to leave the Lutheran Church. His final letter to the Lutheran Church encapsulates his inner state at the time, part of which follows:

> Dear [Bishop]
>
> Through prayer, intense reflection and a desire to submit to the will of God I have come to the conclusion that I cannot, in good conscience, reaffirm the ordination vows that are required later this year to continue in Lutheran ministry. Given my current convictions, I cannot continue to uphold these vows with honesty or integrity. To do so would not be fair to you, to my parishioners, to the Lutheran Church of Australia, nor to myself or my family. Therefore I must ask you to accept this letter as my resignation from the position of pastor of the [local] Lutheran Parish and from the office of public ministry in the Lutheran Church of Australia.
>
> Despite the idyllic setting of my parish, the wonderful people within it, the very positive signs of spiritual growth, and the joy I have in leading these special congregations, I cannot continue to lead and teach people in the way of their salvation when I can no longer believe in that which must be taught according to the Lutheran doctrinal statements.
>
> ... As you are aware, my struggles in the Lutheran Church doctrine have been in various areas – particularly of

> authority and biblical interpretation – and I have prayed and searched hard for solutions for my peace of mind and soul. I believe the only possible answer calls me to return to Luther's own church – the Roman Catholic Church. Although I am sad to leave so many good things, my sadness is deepest in believing that the Lutheran Church has neglected to teach and uphold some of the most profound and wonderful doctrines of the whole Catholic Church ... for the sake my family's souls, and also of my own, we must obey the call of our Lord, and return to His Church ... I hope that those who seek to form opinions on the reasons and motivation for my resignation will do so in mind of the deep grief it causes myself and wife, and that they will take into account the integrity of deciding not taking a vow that I can no longer uphold in good conscience. I pray that the church that I have served and been blessed by in many ways now blesses my parting from it.
>
> Yours in Christ
>
> [Peter Holmes].

Peter also attached a private letter to respond to some of the points raised in recent meetings with his bishop which included the following;

> ... My current stress and emotional distress caused by acting as a Lutheran minister are not just the result of psychological factors; they are the symptoms of a crisis of truth. I believe one thing, and I am called upon daily to live according to another.
>
> ... I believe that the Roman Catholic Church is the true Church. I believe that Christ gave the Church his living authority incarnate in the magisterium and in the chair of St Peter, and that to believe and act otherwise is to reject Christ's own authority and command. I believe that Christ gives His gifts to His Church through the ordained

priesthood handed down by valid succession of bishops. I believe that the sacraments I preside over are, at best, an imitation of the true sacraments.

Finally, if there is any doubt about the strength of my need and desire to return to Rome, if I believe that Rome is the true Church and I do not return to her, my very salvation is in danger. (*Lumen Gentium*, 14)

After the momentous step of resigning from the Lutheran Church, the bishop came over to Peter's house to discuss details of the resignation. Peter recalls that the Lutheran bishop was "sad but seemed almost relieved" and they decided that Peter's final service would be in six weeks.

Telling friends and family

Peter found support among the few Catholic friends he had made and greatly appreciated the fact that no pressure was put on him at any stage. Many of his family, friends and mentors understandably were shocked, hurt, and some were angry. On announcing his resignation to congregations, he choked on the words. He greeted people with tears at his normal place at the door after the service. The congregation were particularly emotional and some even struggled to say anything at all. Deriving great support from his wife, son and daughter he also looked forward to receiving Communion for the first time. That night he wrote, "hold a seat for me at the table, I'm coming home!"

Peter pays tribute in his account to some Lutheran laymen who stayed constant in their support, as did some family members. Fr John Fleming, a convert himself, called and visited when possible. (Then) Fr Anthony Fisher, along with Nicholas and Mary Tonti-Filippini gave much needed gentle and friendly support.

Peter pays especially high tribute to his "darling wife" Susan who "deserves a whole book to acclaim her behaviour and bravery during this period. Our marriage grew much stronger by constant reflection, sharing and shared tears". He views her as "the most dedicated, practical, intelligent, godly and beautiful person I know".

A new life

As a Lutheran pastor he had had an income and a place to live – all of which he had left behind, to follow the light of truth. When the time came to move, a kind Catholic priest put up the bond money for a small house and helped with the big move out of the manse. A week later he had just spent the family's last $16 on fish and chips for dinner on Friday evening and they ate packaged noodles and powdered soup on the weekend. At the eleventh hour, by the intervention of (then) Archbishop George Pell, he was offered a job at Centacare (Catholic Family Services at the time) as an administrative assistant to the Marriage Education Team, a job which gave him time to re-adjust to his new life. He went home to tell his wife and young children that they would eat the following week after all. In the midst of all this Peter and his wife welcomed a new baby into their lives, and named her "Anastasia", meaning "resurrection".

Peter states in his account that he found immense peace in the Catholic Church and pays tribute to his Catholic friends who supported his family spiritually and financially during this difficult period and appreciates the Lutheran friends who stood by him. He says, "I never dreamed of becoming a Catholic, it was the last thing I wanted!" But he recalls being "at peace in mind, body and soul in a way I never felt before. For all its flaws, nuts, heretics, sinners, enthusiasts and idiots (including me) Christ is the head of this house! This glorious, cracked, flawed and complex Church is the only true home for me".

9

From Mao to Catholicism:
an Australian Chinese convert tells her story

This is the story of a woman living in Wagga Wagga who came from mainland China a few years ago to study in Australia. Little did Maylee know of the experiences which she would have here – one of which involved becoming a Catholic. She told me her story during several interviews. Though she first came to Sydney, Maylee has moved to Wagga Wagga as she likes Australian country towns.

Maylee (not her real name) says that she grew up in Mao's China. She was born in Henan province in central China and grew up in a village where she attended the local village school. She was one of five children and all helped out at harvest time and life was frugal and difficult. The way Maylee puts it, in terms of belief, she grew up with nothing. She attended a high school in nearby Wen County and says that at school "we were taught that everything could be explained by science". Anything to do with religion was looked on as superstition and silly. Chairman Mao was the focal point of the world and she was imbued with Marxist indoctrination year after year. Maylee remembers, however, thinking for herself at times amidst the relentless indoctrination. One thought she recalls is that an ant is in its own world and cannot reach out to our human world. She thought maybe we are like ants and cannot reach out to see a greater being outside us. She relates: "When I went outside and watched the sky I felt frightened – I did not know what the sky really was – it was so vast."

Maylee, along with all the other pupils at school, had to join the Red Guard in various exercises and classes. She told me: "We made promises of loyalty to the Chinese government. And then I remember at the age of 10 Mao died and people were so shocked they did not think that China could survive without him." She recalls: "We all cried – Mao was like a god to us." It seemed as if the world had ended and there was no guide to tell people how to live in a post-Mao era.

In the immediate aftermath of Mao's death, Maylee says that villages made floral tributes for him and built statues and monuments. The desire for ritual and to commemorate "forever" was deeply implanted in everyone. Many leaders gave speeches – Maylee says, "We all had to keep silent for three minutes – we were quite terrified as we thought there would now be big problems in China from now on." She says everyone cried, and we felt we could not go on from here. There was continual anguish and there were films of Mao. They watched these films for two weeks night after night. Slogans everywhere said "Mao was higher than the sky and deeper than the ocean." Maylee thought at that time, however, "Where is he now, where is he sleeping if he is not here. Where is he?" Apparently even Mao's China could not suppress some persistent questions from the depths of her mind and soul.

Maylee had never met a Catholic in her life but she still pondered the mysteries of life and death. She was a good student and was able, through her marks, to gain entrance to Henan University. She was the first person in her family to do so and was the source of much family pride. She had to travel to the university and take up lodgings in a student dormitory while enrolling for a science degree. It was here at university she met people who first mentioned the word "Bible" to her – in great trepidation and secrecy. She recalls that during one of the breaks she was sitting with many fellow students around a table in a student refectory and someone mentioned the Bible. She was curious about the word as this was something new for her. Several students asked quietly what this "Bible" was. She said many of them eagerly listened to the student who mentioned it and who seemed to have the answer. This student said that there were books called Bibles in Hong Kong and that sometimes on the radio there were some programmes about it. It was a book containing wisdom. And this book mentioned someone called Jesus Christ who was very wise and extraordinary. All were interested to know what was in this book but not one had ever seen one, apart from the student who mentioned it. She had had some secret Catholic education in her youth. This student who mentioned the Bible said that once upon a time there was a kind of person who used to live in China, who knew all about Bibles and who used to be called a "missionary". The students asked dumbfounded, "What is that?" never having heard this word before either. The student explained that these people were kind, they were called Christians and helped people in hospitals and schools. This student said she had read a book about nuns – and all the students at the table looked at her as if she were an alien coming down from Mars on the first human landing. What was a "nun"? They were fascinated. When she said that they could write to Hong Kong to get a free Bible they all took the address and wrote away to get one. Not one student ever received it, Maylee recalls. Their letters were probably confiscated, Maylee thinks, before they reached their destination or perhaps the Bibles were sent and confiscated before they reached the students. Nonetheless the seed of curiosity had been planted. She had heard the words "Bible", "Christian" and "Christ" but they were mysteries yet to be revealed to her.

A few years later Maylee, having graduated, secured a job in a hospital as a pharmacist specialising in Chinese medicine. The communist system was such that she, along with every other worker, had to attend regular meetings and show enthusiasm for the principles of communism. It was not enough to attend the meetings – one's level of keenness was observed by others at the meetings. She says that well over 90 per cent of the country was well brainwashed in this way.

When the internet era began her interest in other countries was aroused. By this means, and through talking to friends, she formed the idea of coming to Australia, having heard about the courses on offer to overseas students there. So she saved almost all the money from her wages. This involved her not buying food outside the hospital which other hospital workers used to do, as the hospital food was not of very good quality. So she decided to eat only the hospital food and little by little, after several years, she had enough money to pay for her trip to Australia and to do a TAFE course there. Her years of scrimping and saving bore fruit and her wish came true when she arrived in Australia in 2007. She first got accommodation with a Chinese family as a babysitter and then after that finished, she ended up renting a room in Rockdale. She remembers going for a walk one Sunday and while passing a Catholic church thinking "I would like to go inside"; but she was too scared to do so, even though she knew Australia was a free country. She did not know what she was frightened of so she walked past the church and in fact walked around the block on which the church was situated about three times. After the third time she noticed its open door and looked at it from a distance. It happened to be a Sunday and as people entered the gate leading to the church, Maylee followed with a trembling heart, stricken with fear, walking behind them. She said she then stepped inside the church not knowing at that time what a Mass was, but witnessing her first one that day. She recalls, "I was really scared and I just got up and sat down when everyone else did." After Mass she was going to quietly slip away but there was a lady on the porch outside who invited her to have a cup of tea. And that is how she got to know a Filipino lady called Francis who welcomed her and gave her a holy card with St Joseph on it and asked her, guessing that Maylee knew little about Catholicism, "Do you know this is a Catholic church?" Maylee replied, "Yes I know it is a Catholic church and I am interested to talk to someone about it." Francis the Filipino lady said, "If you want to join us come along. I'll be here in the same place at 9.00 am each Sunday." She then gave her a little book of prayers.

Maylee recalls: "I was really excited. All week at my classes I could not wait to get back. I started to think about the Bible. I had read a bit of it in Chinese on the internet. It seemed as if God was always punishing people, that He was like a person. If someone disobeyed him He would punish them." She also thought that God wanted people to be good. Amid a lot of initial impressions, she thought about what she had experienced and the parts of the Bible she had read. She concluded that she liked this religion as the people connected with it were good: "I liked the fact that they had built hospitals and schools and charities and I liked Francis."

She met Francis again, formed a friendship with her and began to think about the big issues: "If I want to believe something I had better believe it deep down." She said she found it difficult to believe as she had been so brainwashed in China. It wasn't that she believed communist propaganda. It was that she was unable to think on a certain level as her brain could not adjust easily to thinking about God as much as she tried to. She came to think in the following way: "So many people want to control us on earth. But really God is the only one really in control of everything." But Maylee did not know how she could imagine or how she should envisage God. She tried to read about it but this attempt to come to grips with a divinely ordered universe was a slow process, although her hunger for understanding was great.

Maylee recounts that before Chairman Mao came along, people thought of God as of a government administration. They prayed to their local gods as there were local animist religions with many gods dealing with every aspect of life. Some prayed every day, some just on festival days and the Chinese New Year. You just talked to someone above although no-one could hear you but yourself and the god to whom you were speaking. Maylee said that her family had not been particularly religious before Mao and so after Mao came to power they just went with the flow. When she went to Mass in Rockdale she observed other people and saw how serious they were. She compared this to Chinese leaders who just pretended to do things for people but who, in her view, were not sincere.

Francis was a friend of Family Life International (FLI), a pro-life organisation with an office in Sydney. She contacted the main office and they contacted me – which is how I came to meet Maylee. John Gresser, then working for FLI, spoke to Maylee with great love and support and suggested she speak to a "counsellor". The reason was that at the same time as her interest in Catholicism was growing, she needed some help in her personal life at that time, as she had been in a relationship with an Englishman after arriving in Sydney and found that she was pregnant. While the Englishman was very keen on the relationship before she became pregnant, he then left her and returned to England. Maylee was having to deal with immense difficulties alone with no family support in a strange country. In fact even being pregnant was against Chinese law so she could not hope for sympathy there. She recalled her sister in China hiding her second pregnancy – literally hiding in a cellar – being betrayed by someone and then being caught by the Family Police. Maylee's sister was forced to have an abortion when eight months into her pregnancy. Before going to the church at Rockdale, Maylee felt very isolated in her difficult situation, but Francis was a wonderful friend in need, as were the people in FLI. Maylee was very open and receptive to the hands of friendship offered to her and people who met her came to know a lovely, thoughtful person with a dry sense of humour. She immediately responded to the view that the unborn child was a human person and all eagerly awaited the birth of her child, even though it was evident that she was in quite a dire situation as regards the future. Maylee came to stay with various FLI people during her pregnancy and there was great rejoicing when her baby son was born. Everyone adopted her child who now had more "uncles" and "aunts" than any other child on earth.

At some point Maylee expressed the wish to know more about the Catholic faith. This was not as easy as it sounds. Her English was good but not up to all that was necessary for instruction. As things turned out she attended her first Christmas Mass at my local parish church – Pagewood's Our Lady of the Annunciation Church, hearing Christmas carols, prayers and seeing a nearby crib in front of which people knelt. During that first experience of Christmas Maylee also went to Maroubra South Shopping Centre and heard Christmas carols sung by school children of the area – along with Little Pattie's guest appearance singing "Stomping at Maroubra". Maylee tried to understand the deep significance of the song but I explained that there was no deep significance – it was just a happy beach song. Maylee absorbed the carols and beach singing as she ate her first pie and sausage roll under the Australian summer sun. It all seemed a bit strange at the time but she persisted in trying to get to the bottom of the mystery.

Sometime later, when speaking to Gail Instance, then director of Family Life International, Maylee learned that there was a Chinese speaking priest that Gail had just heard about in the Priestly Fraternity of St Peter. This priest could speak Chinese fluently so there was great enthusiasm in ringing him. Imagine the puzzlement when everyone learned that the priest spoke Cantonese and Maylee spoke Mandarin, these being very different languages. However the Cantonese priest said, "We are getting a Mandarin speaking member of the fraternity soon and he can instruct her." So one thing led to another with the Mandarin speaking priest arriving soon afterwards. One can ponder long the fact that Maylee received her catechesis from a Mandarin Chinese speaking Latin Mass priest. Maylee did not have any problem with the idea of "Latin" as she knew it was a traditional language of the West, even if she knew little of it. In time she came to love the Latin Mass although she also attended Mass in Mandarin and English.

Sometimes I drove her to the classes in Petersham with the Mandarin Chinese speaking Latin Mass priest. It was on the way there that she would drop bombshells like asking me questions of immense import such as "Why did Jesus die", "Why can't everyone believe in God?" and "What really happened at Christmas?" It is nothing short of thrilling but also a bit terrifying being involved in such discussions with people who are coming to know Jesus for the first time. It is so exciting, indeed a spiritual equivalent of skydiving or climbing Mt Everest, as you never quite know how it is going to go. It is wonderful to see the look in the eyes of the person hearing about Christ for the first time and pondering what she is being told. It is also terrifying as one wants to put the immense realities implied in the questions into the right words. It is like traversing a new land, trying to put into words the contours of a realm of thought one has known all one's life but now has to articulate in a meaningful, coherent way. It is outlining the contours of the greatest mysteries of all and relating the spiritual realities which permeate our existence to an open heart and mind, caring for every step taken. Thank goodness for the priest who could give coherence to the explanations of the great realities and connect it all for Maylee so that she progressed step by step in understanding the universe she had entered. Maylee's Chinese background meant that she had immense respect for those who explained the faith to her and there are many of her compatriots like her.

While she was being instructed in the Catholic faith, Maylee witnessed the crowds of World Youth Day in Sydney in 2008. She travelled a long distance from where she lived to get to Randwick Racecourse to see the Pope arrive by helicopter and to witness the Papal Mass. She was very moved by this amassed witness to the Catholic faith and the evident joy and peace which permeated the immense crowds.

Maylee continued to learn about Catholicism through contact with people, books and thinking about the nature of God, which was always a subject of fascination for her. The upshot of all this and the instruction was that Maylee and her newly arrived baby were both baptised at Lewisham's Maternal Heart of Mary Church in January 2009. It was a very happy Baptism with people who had met Maylee coming from all over the place to be present at the ceremony. She was dressed in white and took Francis as her baptismal name and Rita as her confirmation name (she was impressed by the fact that St Rita is the saint of "the impossible") while Francis and Gail Instance stood behind her and Sydney as godmothers. Young Ronan Reilly looked delighted to be her son's godfather. All watched in awe as Maylee and her beautiful son were baptised and pondered the multiple meetings, connections and mysterious paths that had led to this point.

As time went on, Maylee had to apply for a visa for her baby son. But what kind of visa – was he Australian or Chinese? The Chinese government did not want to know of the 'existence' of this illegal baby and would not register him as Chinese. Nor would the Australian government recognise him as Australian. For a while he was without a nationality, so to speak, but as things turned out, he was eventually granted permanent residence along with his mother some time later. There was a very happy crowd around Maylee when she finally took on Australian citizenship and spoke in terms of immense gratitude about her newly adopted country.

Just think what the friendly invitation to have a cup of tea on the porch of the church at Rockdale led to. Maylee knows she has found the truth and clings to her new faith with the greatest respect and serious attention and has even upbraided a teacher at a TAFE course for joking about Catholics and taking religion too lightly. Maylee could not bear the teacher insulting Catholicism. "It's not right to do so", Maylee said, "and I told her so."

10

Remember who you are

Jocelyn Hedley

Jocelyn is a writer and researcher living in Sydney. She here recounts the spiritual search present from the earliest years of her childhood to the present day. Throughout her life she has listened with an open ear, sensitively, thoughtfully, following the promptings of the spirit, leading her to search for spiritual answers whether working in the theatre, writing or as a journalist. At the time of writing she was engaged in doing a PhD at Notre Dame University in Sydney.

Some years ago, during a very difficult time, I had a sense of losing myself. At one point, the experience was as though I had sunk to the bottom of a deep pool of dark, murky water. There was a sense of constantly attempting to surface, of pushing up through the thickness of water, through the rubbish and reeds, to gain that place of light far above me. When I gained it, I knew, I would begin to be myself again. As I was having this experience, a man stood in front of me, and said the most extraordinary thing to me, over and over, hour after hour: just four little words. *Remember who you are*, he said. *Remember who you are*. I kept looking up to the ceiling, as though to the light of the surface, and then back to his eyes, trying frantically to remember.

It was an extraordinary thing, really. These four little words, like a sonar beaming through the dark depths: *Remember who you are. Remember who you are*. Four little words that worked on me over those hours, and, indeed, over the ensuing years.

The idea that one can *remember* who one is suggests something of continuity, of essence, as though the seed of the self is always present despite interior angst or exterior environment. Even though one may not always remember, or may not remember for many, many years, nonetheless, that self, created and formed in the mind of God, exists. And it is this sense, this sense of remembering, of surfacing, of finding oneself in the mind of God, that is the thread that led me in time to the Church.

I was born in 1966 to an English father and a Scottish mother. My father had come to Australia from Lowestoft, Suffolk, with the Big Brother movement – an organisation founded to encourage British youth migration – when he was 16, and had worked on cattle stations in northern New South Wales and south-west Queensland for ten years before meeting my mother. He was full of stories of a boyhood made romantic by war, and then of a youth as far from the grey coasts of England as it was possible to be. My mother, born during the same war and just newly arrived from Glasgow, was transfixed by his tales of outback adventure – to the degree that she thought she was marrying a farmer.

But my father had left the land behind him. "That's young man's work," he said to me decades later. After a couple of years of marriage and with a secure job in hand, he and my mother moved south to the coastal town of Wollongong, first to a granny-flat in Gwynneville and then to a weatherboard six-roomer in the foothills of Mount Keira just a month before I was born.

When I was two, my mother began to attend the Church of England, and so this is the church in which I grew up. I believed all that I heard of the Good God, and I loved him from the start. One of my earliest memories is of my parents carrying my baby brother and me down the main street of Wollongong. Just beyond what is now the mall, a few young people were gathered together playing guitars and singing Christian songs. My parents stopped and were listening. A man with long hair stepped forward and began to speak with them about God. I was entranced. Every word that he said seemed to be as a brilliant jewel falling from his mouth. I remember leaning forward in my father's arms so as not to miss a thing. I did not want us to go. I wanted us to stay and listen all night. But we did leave, of course. And as we did, the man handed me a tract, the memory of which, even now, evokes within me a strange wondrousness.

At Sunday school I was learning the stories of the Bible and learning, too, to love the Good God more and more. I thought much about him, and longed for a deeper understanding. I knew that God had created the heavens and the earth, and I knew too that He Himself had had no beginning. This concept was a source of great mystery to me, and one which I spent many hours puzzling over. I would lie in bed with my eyes closed and think upon all that I knew of God and of history. It was as though I was stretched out and floating on my stomach with the past events of the world playing out beneath me. The images would rush and tumble, would pass by with great speed. I was always eager for the present to be gone and with it the preceding two thousand years, that I might see all the sooner the biblical times, first the New Testament and then the Old. Back, back I'd go, through the Ascension, the Resurrection and to the Incarnation; further back through the prophets and the kings and the judges. In Eden I would decelerate, take my time over the first words and beginnings and the moving apart of the waters, as though there was some perfect clue previously unnoticed. But then back again, so that what was beneath me was before the creation of the world, was formlessness and void, searching, as I was, ever searching for the beginning of God. And then I would be in the midst of this formlessness, in the midst of this void, with a feeling of incredible frustration that was somehow equally as pleasurable, and with one thought in my mind: that even here before the beginning of time there is no beginning of God.

Then at a Christian camp in the Blue Mountains when I was still quite young, my mother came over to me with much excitement. Come and listen to this, Joe, she said, and drew me towards two men who were deep in conversation. They're talking about God and time, she whispered before moving off. I stood beneath them, a small figure craning upwards, and did not understand a word. But it was a significant moment in that it illustrated for me what I had already been suspecting: that there was much more to God than I was aware of, and much more that it was possible to know.

At eight, things shifted for me when I was diagnosed with encephalitis, an inflammation of the brain tissue. The nature of the illness – and, indeed, of its aftermath – was such that I was plagued by terrifying hallucinations, enough to cause me, at times, to run through the house screaming for my father. Sometimes I was well enough to go to school, sometimes not; and during these latter periods I would lie in my bed and gaze up at the ceiling, which presented itself to me as a bright blue sky. Plainly, my little brain was suffering.

On this particular day I lay in bed with a book in my hands. I was staring at the page without seeing the words when a feeling of both sinking and rising came over me. A moment later and I was up in the corner of my room by the ceiling, looking down upon myself in the bed. At once I was calm and rested. It was lovely up there. I drifted for a while perfectly happy, relieved to be free of the distress of illness for a period. And then, after a bit, I drifted down, and found myself back in my bed and staring at the page before me.

It was not long before I realised that I could float to the ceiling of my room at will, and so, not surprisingly, my illness lightened for me, became less of a burden. My suffering, through what I later understood to be an expression of God's grace, was alleviated, and the ensuing years were easier to bear.

Throughout this time, I would, additionally, experience moments of unexpected and extreme elation. These moments would come unannounced, in the midst of very ordinary activities, would sweep over me in a buoyant, jubilant rush of utter beauty and awe. My breath would be, as it were, snatched from me, and this wondrousness, this astonishing visitation of grace would pour itself into my fibres such that at, the very moment of fullness, I would be likewise pierced, terrified that this would be the last time that I would be so favoured. Each incident was brief, but of so astounding and extraordinary a nature that the memory of it would remain in my body for days. And each time, I would plead: Oh, let this not be the last time. Please let this not be the last time.

These moments were strung across my life as a tension wire: they gave me a taste of the wonder of God such that without them, I felt, existence would be a mere shade. I pictured such a life as of the most extreme greyness, and at times became heavily oppressed by the concept. One day, I stood in the kitchen of our home and, in my mind's eye, saw before me a mass of people. They were all dressed in grey, had grey faces and hair; there was an emptiness to them, a lack of substance that I found terrifying. I was overcome by this image, could not bear the concept that I might become one of the grey masses I saw before me. In my fever and intensity, in my determination not to become like this, I acted foolishly: I lit the stove before me and placed my hand into the flame. I will not be a grey person, I said over and over. I will not be a grey person. I held my hand there for a time, saying these words over and over, with the blue flame licking all the while at my skin. When finally I removed my hand, I held it before me: it was as white and untouched as it ever had been.

When the last of the moments of beauty did indeed come, I was hanging tiny singlets on the washing line for my soon-to-be-born baby brother. I was 12, and as I lifted those small, white garments above me, the unfathomable joy was mixed with a deep desperation: Oh, let this not be the last time! But there was something in the quality of the experience that indicated to me that things would not be as they had been.

A couple of years later, I read C.S. Lewis's book *Surprised by Joy* and was amazed to see something of his experience in my own. I knew the "enormous bliss" he described, and understood, too, what he meant when he said that anyone who has experienced it will want it again. It made me both happy and sad to read this. I was happy that I shared this experience of wondrousness with others, but sad to think that it may not return to me in the manner to which I had been accustomed.

This apprehension of wondrousness, I felt, was of a wondrousness in its pure form. But my Christian and imaginative lives mixed together with literature and tales of fairies and other-world adventures in such a way that there were glimmers of wondrousness all about me, and not infrequently presented by each of my parents: by my father with his unsurpassed story-telling ability, by his invention of enchanting characters and breathtaking scenarios; and by my mother with her involvement in the charismatic movement, and the sense of the extraordinary attendant upon that.

It had been via the Billy Graham crusade in the late '60s that my mother had been drawn to Christianity. In the early '70s, the charismatic revival movement swept through Wollongong, and my mother, though continuing to worship in the Church of England, began to embrace a charismatic spirituality, regularly praying in tongues over my brother and I, and, on occasions, speaking forth words of knowledge. Within this context, I was conscious too of the possibility of modern-day miracles; indeed, my mother herself had been the subject of one of them. While preparing dinner one evening, she prematurely released the lid of a pressure cooker and was immediately covered in boiling liquid and vegetables. She screamed so loudly that a neighbour from half-way down the hill came running up to see what the matter was. She was taken to emergency, and my brother and I to a neighbour's house. We were young, and did not understand the dreadfulness of the situation. We carried our chicken dinner in brown paper bags up the stairs to wait for her return. Sometime later our mother reappeared. Her dress was still wet, but her face was alight. It's a miracle, she said softly, a miracle. The neighbour, a close friend of my mother's, was nodding. Both the neighbour and I were staring at my mother's face, radiant in the dimly lit room. The nature of the accident was such that she should have suffered terrible burns and worn dreadful scars as a result. But there was not one mark upon her.

At 14, I began attending an independent school in Wollongong run by Southern American Baptist missionaries. It was a tiny school, with just 30 students from kindergarten to Year Twelve. Each child sat in their own cubicle, set their own goals for the day and marked their own work. There was a period just after lunch when we would come together as a group, but the rest of the time we worked alone.

The principal of the school was also the pastor of the church and was vociferously anti-Catholic in his beliefs. I hasten to say that this was not something he spoke about with regularity; his business was our spiritual welfare, and this meant instilling the good in us as well as warning us of the bad. Nonetheless, his statements made an impact. I recall the dread and fear that he would rouse in us by announcing that the Catholics were taking over the world. His daughter was my best friend, and we would gasp audibly and exchange looks of horror at the concept. Somehow – through the school? the church? I really can't remember – we got our hands on a series of graphic Chick comics illustrating the evils of the Catholic Church, over which we pored with an endless and morbid fascination.

Catholicism, then, was a great force for darkness and it was we, the true believers, who must be wise to the signs about us, and work all the harder for the salvation of souls. Though it troubles me now that the 'enemy', if you like, was Catholicism, there was much in response to this that I believe was very good. There was a seriousness about the faith and about the work to be accomplished. Though the group was small, its sense of identity was very strong; its definition of itself was formed not only by that which it embraced but, most significantly, by that which it opposed. We were young troops called to battle, equipped with weaponry and sent out into the world to conquer the enemy and to bring salvation to souls. There was absolutely nothing lukewarm about the approach.

I gained much from my involvement with the Baptists, and found their strict codes of conduct very appealing. Though I was participating in Baptist church and school activities, I was still attending the Church of England with my family on Sundays. This was what is now referred to as an Evangelical Anglican church, and though the term itself was not one I was particularly familiar with while growing up, the expressions of it – both in the Anglican and other congregations of which I was later a part – certainly were. I was taught to put little faith in the sacraments (indeed, "sacraments" was a not a word I had heard until well into my 20s), and to ensure that my focus was on a purely personal relationship with God and not entangled in any way with hierarchical authority and mediation. As such, I was, effectively – and along with many, many others – my own Pope, able to interpret the Holy Scriptures for myself and to bypass Sacramental Confession. I was taught that the Eucharist – which we called Communion or the Lord's Supper – was a mere sign, the bread and wine remaining nothing more than simple reminders of Christ's sacrifice. It was abhorrent to consider it any more than this. Should a group of believers decide to enact their own Lord's Supper in someone's dining room and without a minister present, I was free to participate – and I did. My misunderstanding of the place in the Church of Our Lady and of the saints meant that I was bereft of their help, of their consolation and of their friendship. Over many years and across different denominations, I was part of something that – with the accent upon the individual rather than God as agent – was forever trying to reinvent the wheel of "doing church" and to become, as it were, "relevant" to unbelievers. The result was a Christianity that was frequently heartfelt and indeed even vigorous, but just as frequently sacramentally empty, liturgically ad hoc and theologically thin.

Somehow, though, certain elements of this never quite took root with me, most notably my attitude towards the Eucharist. Though I did not think of it as the literal Body and Blood of Our Lord, I had a reverence for the Eucharist and a deep sense of mystery in regard to it that was far greater than that which might have been expected from a mere sign. Anglicans are confirmed at around 14, and are able to receive Communion from this point or shortly thereafter. In preparation, then, for my first Communion, I recall my Confirmation as being, to that point, the happiest day of my life.

All this time, my desire to taste again the wondrousness I had previously known continued to grow. Though I longed for it to be otherwise, church did not seem to be the place where this could happen – not, at least, in the way that I hoped. There had always been for me in the stories of fairies and the little folk a sense of wonder and transport. My reading, then, continued to reflect this as I engaged more and more with works of fantasy and mystical imagination. Alongside this was my interest in theatre, and the sense of a hyper-reality and complete loss of myself that would occur when I performed. To be subsumed in this way was, I found, incredible. Later, when I studied theatre at university, I came across Oscar Wilde's *De Profundis*, and I would refer to it incessantly: art, I would say after Wilde, is the supreme reality, and life a mere mode of fiction. When in Year Twelve I read the part of Tennessee Williams's Blanche DuBois, I became so fixated upon the character that I had to undergo several weeks of counselling in order to de-role.

The reading, the performing: all of this hastened me into other worlds, other lives. All of this subsumed me, took me far from myself, in a way that, though pleasurable, was unbalanced and ultimately harmful. But I was yearning for something. I was trying to find something I had lost. And I was trying to remember who I was.

At 18, a friend who attended a Pentecostal church a few suburbs away was telling me of miracles and speaking in tongues and deliverances from evil spirits. Perhaps, I thought, perhaps I might find something more of the fullness of God in this place. I stopped attending the Anglican church with my family, and started going with my friend to this energetic and frequently dramatic gathering. Here, I experienced everything on offer; and so, when I left Wollongong a few months later to start working in Tasmania, I attended a Pentecostal church in Hobart as well. Might I say that another reason for this was because of something a friend had said; they'd warned me not to go to an Anglican church in Hobart as these, apparently, were more Catholic than anything.

My first job in Tasmania was as a trainee radio announcer and producer at a Christian station in Hobart. We were all home missionaries, and lived by faith. It was an extraordinary year in which I saw the hand of God continuously at work. There was very much the sense of living in a mystical borderland, dependent as we were upon the Lord for all of our needs.

The following year I met two people who would be of great influence upon me. The first was a woman who had not long before converted to Catholicism. I was working at a commercial radio station at this stage, rostered on as the midnight-to-dawn announcer, and we would talk on the phone between my voice breaks for hours into the early morning. My memory is that we only ever talked about religion. She had a seriousness about her that was very appealing; I was deeply impressed when she told me that she had worn a hair shirt for quite some time after her conversion. She took me with her to Mass on a couple of occasions, gave me my first set of rosary beads and introduced me to the teachings of the Catholic Church.

The second person was a radio announcer from our sister station in Launceston. He too would telephone me in the late night hours, and we would embark on long conversations, again about religion. He was a serious and devout Catholic.

When I think back upon this time, it seems quite extraordinary to me. So many very long nights, alone in this building, but kept company by these people telephoning me and speaking with me about religion in general, and about Catholicism in particular. I had other callers, too, listeners: frequently troubled, sometimes just lonely. We all kept each other company in these dark hours, and the recurring theme the night through was religion.

Then a friend from the Pentecostal church offered to take me bushwalking. He was an experienced bushwalker, and thought for my inaugural jaunt that we should go off-track, to a place called the Raglan Range in Tasmania's south west. All well and good, but for the fact that the nature of the bush was far thicker and rougher than we had been expecting. After a couple of days, we realised that we weren't going to make it out on time, and so we began to ration our food. On the Saturday, the day after we'd been expected back in town, it was plain that things were quite dire. By evening, we had eaten very little: just a small amount of milk powder mixed with snow (I'd been trying to make ice cream!) and a few dried apricots. The day had been long and wearying. We had spent a lot of it following a small creek down the slope of the mountain. Occasionally we could hear a helicopter overhead, but that which should have given us hope was in fact a source of frustration to us: we were deep in a seam in the mountain, with a thick canopy of foliage overhead, and a low reach of cloud above that. From where we stood, it seemed as though rescue was impossible.

We trudged on, trying to keep our spirits up by singing and praying and reciting Bible verses. After many hours of this, with our energy plummeting and with the hope of making it out at all growing slimmer and slimmer, I became desperate. I did something that I'd never done before. I, a good Protestant girl who'd been brought up to spurn the idolatry that Catholics supposedly engaged in, did the unthinkable: I prayed to Mary.

I'd never prayed to Our Lady before. Of course I hadn't. And I really didn't know how to do it, what approach I should take. My prayer, then, was very simple. I said only, Mary, would you please pray for us, and could you please get your friends to pray for us too.

A little while later we stopped and pitched our tent. The ground was wet around us; though it hadn't rained, the moisture in the air was dense and cold. We settled in for the night. I began to undertake my usual task of preparing the dinner: tonight just a small handful of rice mixed with a little tomato paste. But, strangely, I felt awkward, unable to perform this simple task. I struggled to stir the billycan and to keep the small candle burning. It all seemed beyond me. When at last I served the meal – just half a bowl between the two of us – I took one small mouthful and felt suddenly not hungry at all. I allowed my friend to take the food, then fell back into my sleeping bag. It was only a moment later that my friend realised I was suffering from hypothermia, and so did his utmost to keep me warm and to keep me conscious. He got me to talk, lying there as I was in my fading state, and my talk, my raving, was all of Our Lady. (But what could I have said? For I knew so very little about her.) And as I fell further and further into darkness, there remained for me a strong sense of a female heavenly presence keeping vigil with me.

In the darkest hour of the night, I woke, conscious that I had made it through the worst, and conscious, too, that it had been with the assistance of she to whom I had prayed that afternoon. I slept again, and when I woke it was morning and I was filled with an incredible peace. Today is the day of my death, I thought, so deeply convinced and so profoundly happy. Today is the day of my death. But the helicopter was searching again and my friend was up a tree trying to attract its attention, and by three o'clock in the afternoon we were airlifted into its hovering belly. And the moment, the very moment, that both of us were safe inside, the mightiest downpour that I have ever seen crashed to the icy earth.

Later, we were told that the week that we were there on the Raglan Range had been the driest on record. It should have been a lot, lot wetter. When I think of that almighty downpour, what do I make of it? That the Good God had kept the clouds from breaking earlier, had spared us the trouble that would have come with the rain? It is not hard to think this. Had it rained earlier in our walk, we would not have been able to get dry, and it is very likely that that Sunday *might* have been the day of my death.

And how much of this did I owe to the intercession of Our Lady? My understanding of such things, though, was yet to come. I praised God for our salvation, and I said a couple of Hail Marys with my Catholic friend, but my life in Pentecostalism hadn't yet paled. Later it would, and I would begin in earnest the journey through the many different Protestant churches that would become the outworking of my search for this unknown something deeper, for this taste again of something transcendent. But at this point, the energy and excitement of the Pentecostal church were answering to something.

It was the liturgy that brought me back to the Anglican church. If I had found it thin in the past, then I had found other modes of worship far thinner. The Pentecostal and Charismatic style no longer attracted me; I found the experience of constantly whipping myself up into some sort of faux ecstasy dissatisfying and hollow. I didn't feel a depth here. I didn't feel the presence of God. I came to loathe the lack of beauty in the surroundings, to find unbearable the plastic chairs and the stark, stripped stage devoid of any sign of an altar. I yearned to hear a sermon about something more than how I could have my sins forgiven if only I believed in Jesus. I was hungry; I was starving. I knew I wanted something more but I still didn't know what it was, or where I could find it. I just knew that it wasn't this, and it wasn't here.

At least in the Anglican church, I felt, there was some sense of order and direction. But, even so, I could never stay in the one church for very long. Whenever I started at a new church, there was always the longing that this would be it, that here I would find what I was looking for. But time would prove otherwise, and I'd feel just as frustrated and empty as ever – and be blighted by horrific headaches that would send me to bed for the rest of each Sunday. I was aware that on the outside I looked like a church-hopper, like one who was not serious. But the opposite was the case: I was very serious.

By now, I was beginning to consider ideas that would be of key importance in terms of my eventual conversion: the doctrines of transubstantiation and apostolic succession. As I spent more and more time in Anglicanism, these teachings began to mean something to me; I could not take them lightly. In some ways, they caused me great pain, because, despite my to-ing and fro-ing, my attachment to the Anglican church ran deep; I considered her my mother. Yet, these issues nagged at me, and would not let me rest.

During this time, I was writing my first book, a story of a young woman who decides to end her life by a very particular means, and in the process of researching this means, discovers worlds she had not known existed. She realises, then, that she knows little of either life or death, and so begins a journey to discover more of both, such that her decision to live or to die might be a more informed one. She seeks out experts in each of these areas – and one of these experts is a mystic.

It was the writing of this chapter that led me to mysticism, and to Christian mysticism in particular. I began to read works by any number of mystics: by Walter Hilton and Richard Rolle; by Saints John of the Cross and Teresa of Avila. I read *Revelations of Divine Love* and *The Cloud of Unknowing*. I was introduced to the Philokalia, and to *The Way of the Pilgrim*. I read here of the Jesus Prayer, and began at once to say this simple, astonishing prayer: "Lord Jesus Christ, have mercy on me". I started to find myself with the prayer seeping into my blood, and it was a deep and wondrous joy to me.

I read and I read. I filled every part of myself with these works and with the writers of these works. They were Catholic and Orthodox people, and in the midst of this, not surprisingly, my thoughts pertaining to Catholicism began to take on a new and radiant hue. I began now to speak with the saints, to beseech the intercession of Saints Francis and Clare. (And how lovely that it is St Francis of Assisi's church in Paddington in which I now worship!) I would walk long tracts through the park, conscious of the enormity of things and imagining myself surrounded by a great cloud of witnesses, all of us walking together and saying those simple words as one: "Lord Jesus Christ, have mercy on me". That prayer, without question, drew me yet closer to the Church; and the intercessions of those saints with whom I was speaking likewise called down God's graces upon me.

My life, at this point, effectively changed – wholly and unexpectedly. There was an emerging wonder, a deep satisfaction; something in me was being met, was being answered. Some part of me was remembering, was surfacing. I became at this time particularly devoted to Saint John of the Cross, and was deeply affected by his poem *Dark Night of the Soul*. As I immersed myself in all of these works, I began to see more and more of the mystical present to me in everyday life, of the wonder and joy of all things in union with God. It was an extraordinary time: of understanding; of oneness; of euphoria; of love. The overwhelming outworking of all of these things – the reading, the experiences, the contemplation – was, indeed, that of love: love in the awareness of God in all things and all things in God that is love. My perception of everything shifted, deepened, brightened, heightened. It was as though I was being slowly subsumed, absorbed; slowly conquered, overwhelmed. And my movement towards the Church was only nearer and nearer.

The last church that I attended before my conversion was a High Anglican church where the doctrine of the Real Presence was held to, homilies about angels were given and the dead prayed for. I saw a richness here, a beauty and a surge towards profundity. By now, after engaging with the lives of these mystical saints and discovering a growing appreciation of the Church in which they were formed and nourished – and beginning to comprehend the teachings of the Church which I had previously *completely* misunderstood – Apostolic Succession meant something to me. And as for transubstantiation – well, I realised one day during the Eucharist that I believed this most wonderful truth; and when this clarity in my understanding and change in my heart occurred. I realised too that I could no longer *not* be a Catholic. I knew that I had to convert.

When, on that truly happiest of nights – Easter Vigil 2004, at St Patrick's, Church Hill – I received for the first time the true Body and Blood of Our Lord, not only did I become a member of that mystical union that is the Catholic Church, and indeed experience an almost physical comprehension of this, but something else happened; something in me quietened, drew back. That hungering, that starvation, was immediately sated; and that yearning for mystical transports and euphoria grew dim – for the fullness of all things was here.

All my life, I had struggled to remember who I was. I had lived an autonomous existence, devoid of the fullness of communion and fractured because of it. But I had always by God's grace been drawn to search for that which was missing, for that which I only dimly remembered. And all of these things I finally and fully found in the mystical communion of the Catholic Church.

And there in the quietness of the Mass, in the participation in the Body and Blood of Our Lord, I finally remembered who I was meant to be.

I was meant to be a Catholic.

11
From temples and mosques: once a Sufi, now a Catholic

Toshiko Hitchings, who lives in Sydney and is Australian though Japanese by birth, relates a interesting conversion story which spans several continents. I interviewed Toshiko in May 2009, after we met outside following Mass at the Sacred Heart Church in Randwick. Toshiko was happy to tell of her long journey via Buddhism and Sufi Islam, to Catholicism. (Interviewer questions are in bold italics).

Tell us a bit about yourself Toshiko.

I was born in Japan in Kakogawa city near Kobe. I was educated at Kakogawa High School and became a pharmacist there. My family were Jodo Shinshu Buddhists, which means they followed literally the "Pure Land Sect" sect of Buddhism. This was a movement in Buddhism which was founded by the monk Shinran Shonin (1173-1263) who was a pupil of the revered monk Honen, a reformer who simplified Buddhism and focused on recitations to the Buddha Amida, saying things such as "Namu Amida Butsu" meaning "I take refuge in Amida Buddha."

What were your first thoughts of a spiritual nature?

Well, my family followed the rituals of Jodo Shinshu Buddhism, without knowing too much about it in the way that some people practise their faith, without knowing too much about its beliefs. When my great grandmother died, she was burned in a Buddhist ceremony, and I remember asking myself "Where is she going?"

I went with my grandmother to the temple and over the years I also recall having some vague idea of future joy in going to meet Buddha.

During high school, I had a pen-friend – having a pen friend was popular in Japan – and this friend was actually a Muslim who wrote to me about Islam and introduced me to the idea of fasting and prayer. This had a great impact on me. After I finished high school, I went to a Pharmacy College and one of my subjects was anatomy. I remember seeing dead people in this class and thinking that the "soul", as I understood it then, was gone and wondering where it went. I thought the human being was not just a body but a unity of body and spirit. I was interested in reading various holy books, which I did from time to time.

What did you do after you finished your studies?

Well I wanted to go to travel somewhere. One idea was that I would be a volunteer somewhere in India and use my skills there. In my family, we were used to the idea of travelling as my father actually belonged to the Lions Club and had organised for my brother to go to Australia on exchange for a while and an Australian boy came to our house in 1971, also on exchange, and so I heard about Australia.

In any case I ended up going to Australia in 1972 and went on a cruise. On my way home I stopped in Hong Kong, Taiwan and Papua New Guinea. On that ship I met my husband, Patrick Hitchings, the ship's doctor, who was from New Zealand. He had been born a Catholic but had converted to Islam and he had many books and I was able to ask him many questions about his beliefs. At that time I did not agree with the use of the contraceptive pill and he agreed with me as we both thought it was harmful to the body. We used to discuss topics such as what was harmful to the immune system and what was not. We married not long after and I became more and more interested in Islam

What did you do then?

Then life became very interesting. My husband Patrick and I went to Iran, which at the time was under the rule of the Shah of Iran. The reason is that my husband was very interested in Sufi Islam and went to meet a master of Sufism – Seyyed Hossein *Nasr*. This master lived in Teheran and invited my husband to work as a doctor in a small village called Aleshta which is in the middle of Iran. I recall there being no running water, no electricity and very pure air and beautiful stars at night. I didn't mind. While we lived there my husband studied Sufi Islam and at some point was initiated to Sufism by Nasr. He would have to meditate for a long time and I became very interested in all this and about a year later I became a Sufi as well.

A great master of Nasr, Frithjof Shuon, actually lived in Switzerland at the time. He was Swiss and had come from a Protestant and Catholic background to Sufism. He had studied in Egypt and had founded a Sufi order and returned to his country. So we went from Iran to learn from him in Switzerland. I was 26 then and we were invited to come to pray with this Sufi master and his disciples. Sufi ladies helped me with understanding Sufism and taught me how to follow my husband's prayers reciting a "Mother Mary" prayer. One of the prayers I said a lot at that time was to "Mother Mary", yes, really, it was to the "Virgin Mary". Of course, our prayers also involved invoking Allah without ceasing. However, even though I prayed, I felt God was far from me. I used to meditate for a long time too and say special prayers.

During my prayers at the initiation to Sufism I had a kind of dream or vision – something like a 'mental vision' without opening my eyes. I saw a gold shining figure and I walked through Golden pillars towards this figure and entered into his body. I felt the pillars as "pillars of prayer" which I should build with each passing day. We returned to Iran and despite our keenness to learn more spiritually, in 1976 we felt we had to leave Iran as the revolution was looming. We knew that another master of our Sufi order, Martin Lings, lived in England. As my husband's father was English, we could stay in England without a visa at that time and so we decided to go here. On the way we visited Maryamana (Mother Mary's house) in Ephesus in Turkey. There was hardly any one there as this was a time when few people came to see Ephesus I think. My husband and I prayed there together – to Mary – as we had wanted a child and had not yet had one. Six months later I became pregnant. At that time, my husband was looking for work but could not find any in England and so he then decided, after a while, to accept an offer of a job in Saudi Arabia. We went there in 1977 and that was where my daughter was born. We called her "Maryam" as we felt that "Mother Mary" in Ephesus had answered our prayers for a child. My husband worked in the military hospital at Khamis Mushait, a city in southwest Saudi Arabia, near Yemen. We were there for over two years. Then tragedy struck. My husband had a massive heart attack at the age of 56 and died. Our daughter was only two years old. It was an immense shock and I had to plan what to do.

What did you do after your husband died?
I could not stay in Saudi Arabia so I had to decide what to do. My parents said they could look after my daughter so I returned home and lived with them in Japan.

This is strange but when I returned I did not see any difficulty with returning to Buddhism as I thought all spiritual paths led to wisdom and so I turned back to the faith of my childhood. I had also begun to feel very guilty about not keeping up with the five times of daily prayer and more in Sufism and not being able to fast as often as required. Back in Japan I started to read books about Buddhism again at home – it was easier for me to read about these beliefs in Japanese, after trying to grapple with Arabic and the Sufi prayers. As a Buddhist I could see that Buddha Amida is merciful and spoke of mercy to the sinner. Mercy was very much in my mind then and I pondered this quality in the Buddha. I became involved again with my spiritual reading and went to Kyoto, the home of Jodo Shinshu. There is a big temple there and I often did three days' retreats during which we were told about how we are attached to pride and self-centredness, and that by the mercy of Buddha Amida, we could be released from this. Reflecting on the quality of mercy gave me great consolation.

Then, as my daughter grew up, I realised that she should learn English. As I said before, my family were accustomed to travel. My brother was a diplomat and travelled quite a bit. I decided to go to New Zealand where we could stay, because of my deceased husband's being born there. My father said he could help us financially if we went there. We went to Wellington when my daughter was 13 and my daughter became fluent in English as well as Japanese and continued her education there. We had to get used to living there and taking care of ourselves. Somehow we managed with all the difficulties we had.

So how did you find a way to delve more deeply into the Bible?
I looked for a Buddhist temple to attend in Wellington but I could not find one. Then by chance I met an Anglican priest who invited me to come to a Bible study in Japanese. I was a bit confused as it is hard to go to something like that if you are an outsider. But I went along and listened and attended some sessions. I was attracted

to the teachings of the Bible and was interested in what I heard. After I finished the course, someone asked me, "Why don't you become a Christian?" I thought about this for some time without answering. I did want to do spiritual reading and study because that is what my nature sought all the time. I could not find a Buddhist temple to go to so I thought, "Maybe, God is calling me in a new direction". In any case, I continued with my studies and decided to be christened at the Lady's Chapel in 1997 in an Anglican church in Wellington in 1997. However, although I was happy with this, I felt I was missing something and looking back, it was devotion to "Mother Mary". There was no such devotion with the Anglicans, as good as they were, and I felt I could not grasp the Bible in the way I wanted to. I wanted to understand it more deeply.

Then another day in Wellington I was walking along the road when I saw a sign outside another church saying "Adult Education Centre." It was outside a Catholic church and there was a sign advertising study of the Bible, the Old Testament and the New Testament. I felt an urge to study Christianity further. I went to the classes which were run by Fr Edmond Little who had studied in Israel. He knew Hebrew and could tell us a lot about Jesus and the Bible, so I learned a lot from going there. He was very logical and could explain the answers to questions. He was strict – we had to start exactly on time. I really learned a lot.

I recall thinking that the Bible is not only remembrance about the past but also about the present, that the Old Testament is related to the New Testament. I got used to thinking about Jesus. Father Little asked me at some point, "Would you like to become a Catholic." I did not know what to say as I did not want to go along with what I thought was a "denomination" – I just wanted to be Christian. So I said I would think about it. After finishing the course I was still thinking about it.

So, how did you find your way to becoming a Catholic?

At that time, because I was interested in the prayer of the rosary, I asked a Filipino lady whom I met at the church, what it was about. She said, "I'll teach it to you." She invited me to come to the Legion of Mary meetings held at the church where they said the rosary, and so I learned to say it. I went along to the Legion and even though I was not a Catholic they welcomed me warmly. There, a lady used to tell me about Our Lady and about apparitions – Fatima, Lourdes, Medjugorje, and so on. After all this, I decided I really wanted to become a Catholic. I told a priest – Father Berry – I wanted to convert to Catholicism and he led me to the RCIA course. But the course was quite a long way from home and when Father Berry realised that, he said, "I can give you a private course." And so it happened, I had a private course, and in 2001, in the Sacred Heart Cathedral in Wellington, I became a Catholic and am happy in my faith to this day. After my conversion I went on a pilgrimage and, among other places, I visited Medjugorje with my daughter and while we were there my daughter announced to me that she also would like to become a Catholic. "I want to become a Catholic daughter", she said. So my daughter also became a Catholic. Interestingly, I thought that at Medjugorje I would become closer to Our Lady, but I got much closer to Jesus, especially when I climbed Mount Krizevac, where the cross is at the top. We had many deep spiritual experiences there and I feel so much closer to Jesus and our mother Mary. I came to a deeper understanding of the Eucharist and I remember that wonderful moment when I said, "The Eucharist (transubstantiation) is really true."

And now?

I always feel that my life has been a strange journey with so many different paths but that I have been very blessed. I have found my spiritual home and want to stay in it forever. I thank God for blessing my life, for the blessings that were already there behind my husband's prayers. I have great peace in coming to Mass and in praying the rosary regularly.

My daughter got married and was living in Australia so I came to Australia to live close to them. I have two grandchildren and one of them goes to St Margaret Mary's school in Randwick. I go to Mass every day at the church next to this school and at Our Lady of the Sacred Heart in Randwick.

What would you say to "cradle Catholics"?

I would say that I want them to appreciate the beauty of the Mass. The Eucharist is an extraordinary gift from God, the most extraordinary of all that I have encountered in my life. Also, I think it is very important to keep an open mind and heart in life, and leave everything in God's hands. If you are open to God, God definitely guides you to His Heart and gives you inner peace and happiness. God works mysteriously all throughout our lives.

12
From gay Marxist to Catholic: the story of Christopher Pearson

Renowned journalist Christopher Pearson found his way through the century's radical belief systems and ideological minefields to the Catholic faith. Formerly a Marxist, he regarded his newly found Catholicism as his greatest treasure.

Christopher Pearson, one of Adelaide's most famous sons, was actually born in Sydney on 28 August 1951, to Robert Forster Pearson and Sidney Suzanne Dutton. He spent most of his life in Adelaide, however, becoming well accustomed to its artistic ambience, its literary vitality, not to mention its political commotions and controversies. After attending Scotch College, he received a Bachelor of Arts with Honours from Flinders University, with French and English among his subjects, as well as gaining a Graduate Diploma in Education from the University of Adelaide.

Pearson was an only child who from an early age showed a distinct inclination to reading and literary pursuits, though his interests ranged far afield and included music, languages, history and politics. His parents separated when he was quite young but always encouraged their literary, scholarly son who by his own admission read encyclopaedically. Pearson's father was a former IBM manager but then entered the Anglican ministry and his mother had numerous artistic interests and was a general supporter of the arts. Though Pearson says he became a Marxist at age 10, he did try to share some of his father's interest in Christianity, being attracted to the prayer and music of church services. In the end, however, it was the radical *zeitgiest* of the era, the ferment of student politics, the overwhelming belief in the infallibility of human progress that won over any nascent Christianity. This happened to so many intellectuals of the era and the powerful influence of Marxism on young minds is described in several works such as David Horowitz's *Radical Son: A Generational Odyssey* (1998).[7] He was influenced by the views and persona of South Australia's Premier Don Dunstan who was a iconic figure to the intellectual *bon vivants* and progressives of Adelaide during that era. Pearson declared himself a homosexual as a young man and was linked with many high profile Adelaide gay activists such as the eminent jurist and poet John Bray. In short, Pearson became one of Adelaide's many radical sons, one of the leftist glitterati, sharing dreamscapes of utopian futures while adding an incisive wit and literary talent to all he did.

Going into journalism seemed a natural progression for Pearson's verbal talents and investigative proclivities. As a journalist Pearson had many notable successes in his early forays into disputed matters, bringing the Hindmarsh Island Affair and the South Australian State Bank disaster to prominent national attention. He was the founding editor of *The Adelaide Review* and eventually became a long-term columnist for *The Australian*.

A tendency to "look at the other side" and to questioning himself and others gave him a breadth of interests. It also gave him a capacity to look further into questions than the prevailing political correctness might allow. Pearson went his own way, fearless as to the political and ideological consequences. This may have been the underlying quality that suggested paths beyond the radical wilderness and may have sparked his search for enduring realities beneath the enigmas of life and eventually his journey to Catholicism. Pearson was not afraid to question cherished views, nor himself. Evident from those who knew him, he was open to critiquing the world views of those he met, as if seeing through apparent truths but searching for a deeper reality beneath the appearance of things. Thus, although he was reputed to have been a Keating supporter at one stage, he also talked to conservatives – always searching, always questioning, always engaging and riotously witty. Tony Abbott with whom he became friends says of Pearson:

> In some ways, ours was an unusual friendship: he had begun life on the political Left, I was an instinctive conservative; he was the cultivated aesthete, I was the extrovert politician; he regarded Palestrina as the prince of music, while my only musical king was Elvis Presley. But he was intellectually curious and a lifelong seeker-out of people from whom he thought he might learn.[8]

After several years of the radical lifestyle lived in full Adelaidean splendour, something was stirring within Pearson. To the horror of several contemporaries he began to question his radical beliefs and was less than happy with what he saw in his radical colleagues, including the previously unassailably wonderful Don Dunstan. He stated that, like Keynes, "When the facts change, I do change my mind." Pearson said the following:

> We once had a rather endearingly old-fashioned Fabian sort of premier. He became less and less Fabian and more and more concerned with consolidating his position in the new class and feather-bedding any number of apparatchiks. He sold out to the "greed is good brigade". The sad thing was he took on their moral values uncritically.[9]

He befriended a priest Fr Ephraem Chifley who shared many of his interests both literary, historical and culinary, though Pearson says he was initially wary of Chifley for "fear he might attempt to convert him". However, Fr Chifley reputedly laughed this off saying, "It was obvious to me that he was seeking conversion one night in the Universal Wine Bar. He was denying the Holy Trinity, that's always a giveaway. People don't usually go out of their way to deny the recherche aspect of Christianity. Once you do that you're on the way."[10]

Indeed Pearson was on the way, and saw his earlier forays into Anglicanism as attempts to find some certainty. For, unlike what his friends said, it was not simply beauty he yearned for (and this always was in him) but far and above this it was the "certainty: immutable doctrine and valid sacrament". He thought deeply about the deeper issues. Even his homosexuality was not immune from his relentless scrutiny. On this matter, when reflecting on his journey to Catholicism he said:

> There was no getting around the fact the New Testament said we were all meant to be chaste or monogamously married and I had reluctantly concluded that St Paul was right about homosexual sex.[11]

He realised he could never have been happy as a "gay Christian – with or without a rainbow sash" because it "seemed a contradiction in terms". His desire for clarity propelled him to understand that the Bible did not have mixed messages, though some of what it says has been variously interpreted. He knew there was a point of no return if he were to accept the Church's teachings on homosexuality – and he eventually did accept them.

In the process of searching for the deeper realities, he had recollections of that subtle yet enticing peace that passes all understanding which he sensed dimly in his youth before the turbulent influences of young adulthood swept him away. A desire for this peace evidently never quite left him, as ebullient, insatiably curious and witty as he was. In his own account of his journey to Catholicism, he pondered the filaments of memory and eventually he came to look at his life in a different way, saying that he realised there seemed "nowhere else to go". The monumental realities of Christianity stared him in the face, one by one. They could not be argued away – they remained after all the words were said and the counter arguments flung against its bastions again and again. Pearson came to the conclusion, however, that he could not accept the changing doctrines of the Anglican Church and that fact that "Anglicanism was beset by strange, divisive fads".[12]

He had read John Henry Newman's *Apologia Pro Vita Sua* at age 17, and now coming back to this, Pearson saw that this work "mounted a powerful argument that the only way the Reformation churches could sustain their preferred versions of their institutional identity was by systematically ignoring most of ecclesiastical history, especially the more inconvenient aspects of the early Church and patristic theology". He was increasingly drawn to the stability of Catholic doctrine which remained despite the weaknesses of the Church's individual members. He came face to face with the Catholic world view and its sacraments, in particular the sacrament of confession or reconciliation:

> Making a commitment to regular examination of conscience was unexpectedly therapeutic, It led me to trade in my double bed for something more austere, observe the Lenten fast and try, for the most part to avoid low bars. I read again the *Confessions* of "Augustine of Hippo" who had famously prayed "Lord, make me chaste, but not yet" and knew how he felt.[13]

Pearson's conversion was understandably a shock to his radical comrades who could not understand that someone so intelligent and witty, a Maoist, a committed radical, could not only become a conservative who had the time of day for people like John Howard as well as Mark Latham, but also could enter the strange territory of Catholicism. Pearson who once delighted the Bollinger bolshies now was "loathed by large sections of those on the Left of politics".[14] Jacquelynne Wilcox, who remembered him as a friend and mentor, recalls, however, that South Australian Attorney General Michael Atkinson went against the grain and kept his friendship with him. He sought Pearson out saying "He's hated and that's one of the reasons I like to spend time with him ... the idea of some Left liberal like Christ Schacht spewing that I've been seen having lunch with Christopher Pearson appeals to me. It's dangerous."[15]

Pearson's conversion to Catholicism did not blind him to the fact that there were problems within the Church. He knew that converting was not going to be a "bed of roses". After going to great pains to understand what the Catholic Church taught, he noted the lack of a sense of sin, the lack of understanding of the legacy of the Church's immutable doctrine, the woeful state of preaching in some sections of the Church. Despite all, he came to understand, as did Flannery O'Connor, that "the Church is the only thing that is going to make the terrible world we are coming to endurable" and that "it seems to be a fact that you have to suffer as much from the Church as for it".[16] He found O'Connor and Malcolm Muggeridge kindred spirits in his journey. Being attracted to the traditional music and prayers of the Church and especially to the Latin Mass, he felt as marginalised and persecuted as the first generation of gays and so felt as if he were reliving his radical days in a certain sense.

It seems no matter what Pearson did, he would always have to search his way into the heart of mystery before him, drawing upon his prodigious knowledge and wide horizons of activity. Before and after his conversion to Catholicism, he always remained involved in many spheres of society. He was a member of the Council of the National Museum of Australia and also on the board of the government-owned SBS television station. In addition, he served as a speech writer to the former Prime Minister of Australia, John Howard, and gave invaluable advice to many aspiring journalists.

He wrote for the *Herald*, *The Age*, and *Courier Mail* among other news outlets. He seemed to be in good spirits on 9 June 2013 when he lunched with friends in Adelaide and then returned home to his Hurtle Square home.

No-one could have suspected that this was to be the last day of Christopher Pearson's life on earth. He was only 61. He must have died alone some time after returning home. He did not turn up for Mass the next day and this raised the alarm. His friends and foes felt acutely the passing of this radiant star, transmitter of joy and yet utter seriousness, and an extraordinarily lively thinker. What mattered for him most in the end as an irrepressible seeker for the truth was what lay beyond the horizons of the visible world.

13

From Japan with love: how Kanae became a Catholic

This conversion story is the narrative of a journey from Japan to Australia, a new life and a new religious faith. Kanae Micallef came here on holiday, decided "this is the place I want to live" and moved here, little knowing that this was the place where she would get married and become a Catholic.

Sharyn McCowen

Kanae Micallef was born in Japan and made the big move to Australia in 2003.

Recently she made another big move when she was baptised a Catholic at the Easter Vigil at St Mary's Cathedral.

"I grew up in Chiba, Japan – it's just next to Tokyo – with my parents and my sister," Kanae said. "My sister is 13 months older than me."

Like many Japanese, Kanae's parents are nominally Buddhist but don't actively practise their faith. "I think most Japanese are Buddhist but most of them actually don't believe anything," she says. "They are Buddhist, but they don't have a strong faith. This is quite normal. When I was a child, I think I was a tomboy, because my neighbour had only boys. I never played with dolls; I always preferred roller-skating or riding a push bike."

Kanae attended a private girls' school, which she enjoyed "very much", especially studying maths. "That school isn't connected to any religion, so I didn't have any opportunity to learn religious subjects. But I really enjoyed school." After high school, Kanae studied fashion design for three years, a far cry from [being] the tomboy of her youth. But the course and, ultimately, the industry failed to capture her interest, and Kanae began working for a hotel. While there, she befriended a colleague with an Australian boyfriend.

When the colleague invited Kanae to join her on a holiday to Australia late in 2000, she jumped at the opportunity. "I came with her, for 10 days or so," she recalls.

"I always wanted to live overseas, and I had had a few travel experiences before that, to Canada, the United States, New Zealand and Hong Kong.

"I have to choose English-speaking countries, but even in those countries I couldn't see my future there. I just felt like a tourist." But Australia was different.

It was here that she had the realisation: "I want to live here! This is the place I want to live". Kanae explains: "The weather was beautiful. People are so friendly, kind and relaxed. I felt comfortable. My first few overseas trips were secret from my parents. This is because my parents were not so flexible when it comes to living overseas; they thought it was too dangerous! I didn't have much doubt or physicality in making the decision [to move]. I had the logistical problems of the language barrier, how can I get a visa, how can I live there, how can I get a job. It was difficult but somehow everything worked out well. I think I was very lucky."

Kanae had made a promise to herself that she would move to Australia within two years, and she made it just past her deadline, returning in January 2003. She started work as a customer service consultant for a financial company, a role she held for six years.

In 2005 Kanae met lawyer James through mutual friends at

the Marble Bar one Friday night. While both acknowledge an immediate connection, it was James' choice of drink that left the biggest impression on Kanae.

"He drank tomato juice in the Marble Bar! What a strange guy," she says.

"He was very polite, he was very gentle, but Friday night, tomato juice at the Marble Bar?"

Kanae was later reassured that James' choice of drink was because he was driving.

They began dating soon after.

Though he didn't talk about faith early on, James allowed Kanae to experience the Church through occasional trips to Mass and her deepening relationships with his Catholic family and friends.

"Near the beginning of our relationship, we went to church together," Kanae recalls.

"His parents, Louis and Antonia, have a strong faith. My first impression of his mum, who is my godmother, is that she was a very trustworthy person and often I thought: 'She must be a saint'. Even now I often think that."

James' childhood friend Angelo also set a great example. "He is of Italian background and he also has a strong faith, and is a very sincere guy."

They were married on 13 May 2007, in the Cardinal Cerretti Memorial Chapel at Manly, with Sydney on display for Kanae's family from Japan.

It was her parents' first trip to Australia, her mother's first ever trip overseas, and they enjoyed seeing the sights and getting to know the Micallefs. "They loved James and his family, and that was very important," she says.

As part of their pre-marriage preparation, Kanae committed to raising any children in the Catholic faith: "I wanted to raise my children to be Catholic."

Two years ago Kanae discussed with James the idea of becoming a Catholic. He was eager to make sure she was choosing the faith for the right reasons, for her own beliefs, not just because of him. They continued to discuss the idea, and were spurred on when Kanae became pregnant. Unbeknown to the couple, James' mother Antonia had been praying daily for some time that James and Kanae would have a baby and that Kanae would become a Catholic.

Already ecstatic at the pending arrival of their grandchild, James' parents were both thrilled when Kanae called and asked Antonia to be her godmother.

"When I told my mother-in-law she was so happy," Kanae says. "She was speechless."

Kanae started attending the weekly RCIA (Rite of Christian Initiation for Adults) meetings at St Mary's Cathedral in January. "The first time I was a bit nervous, but it gave me a lot of knowledge of Catholicism and they were such nice people, very helpful."

On 7 April, she was one of five women who received the sacraments of baptism, confirmation and communion for the first time. "That was more special than I thought," she says.

"I thought it would be more simple, that I would go to the local church for the sacraments with no one really interested. But it took place at the Easter Vigil at St Mary's Cathedral with Cardinal Pell presiding and all our family came to the ceremony that day."

Kanae was a "little bit" nervous about her sacraments taking place before a full congregation at the cathedral, including 19 members of James' family, but she drew excitement and strength from them.

"The family was so excited about it, much more than I thought," she says.

As James accompanied Kanae through the RCIA process, he experienced a revival of his own faith. He learned from the classes, but also shared his own experiences as a Catholic with other catechumens.

The couple are parishioners at St Leonard's and attend Mass each week. At the time of writing, Kanae was eight months' pregnant, with "24-hour sickness" long behind her and enjoying her pregnancy. She and James are eager to welcome their first child, a baby girl.

"She's a very good girl," Kanae says. "I think I must be truly blessed, because now I can raise this baby as a good Catholic parent in the Catholic faith.

"I also hope to have more children, God willing."

Kanae is still a keen traveller, and has enjoyed using Sydney as a base to explore other parts of Australia, with visits to Victoria, South Australia, Western Australia, the Northern Territory, the ACT, the Blue Mountains and Byron Bay. She would like to see Tasmania, and also plans to visit her family in Japan with her daughter.

"I love spending time with our family."

This story has been printed with kind permission of Sharyn McCowen and the Catholic Weekly.

14

Certainty mattered in the end

John lives in northern Queensland with his wife Marea (not their real names). He was born in England, graduated from Oxford University, lived in Africa as a young man and was Anglican for most of his life. Loving the peace and sunshine of the Antipodes, he migrated to Australia when he was in his 40s. Little did he know that, in coming here, he would set in train the events that would lead to his conversion to Catholicism. This is his story given during an interview with me. Interviewer questions are in bold italics.

What made you think of converting to Catholicism?
When I think back, it was not so much a conversion as such from being an agnostic, Muslim or Buddhist. You see I was an Anglican, but not a very committed Anglican, so I kind of drifted along without any strong beliefs for quite a few years. What changed me was meeting a lovely Australian woman (whom I married in the end) for whom the faith mattered a great deal. Marea came from a very Catholic background. She was truly a cradle Catholic of Irish-Australian background and the faith had deep roots in her. And because of this I wanted to know what she believed. So it was a person more than the ideas which attracted me and so I decided to go to the RCIA (the Rite for the Christian Initiation for Adults). There were no particular points that I was searching for. My Catholic friend said that if she ever married it would be in a Catholic church as marriage was a sacrament. As time went on and I got to know her better, I realised I had to understand what she was talking about. For to understand a person you need to understand what they think, they believe, they love.

I had no objection, if one can put it that way, to trying to find out. So I ended up enrolling in RCIA classes in St Brigid's parish in Coogee [in Sydney – Ed.].

How did you find what the RCIA said?
Many of the beliefs of course are the same. For instance both Anglicans and Catholics believe in Christ and the resurrection. However when it comes to the question of the forgiveness of sins I found that the Catholic Church was more certain and positive than in the Anglican Church. I inevitably came up against the issue of the primacy of the Church. Which was the Church that Christ founded? I realised as the RCIA classes went on that the Anglican Church really was a breakaway from the Church Christ founded. I learned that the Archbishop of Canterbury was a political appointment which I had never before realised as an Anglican. I came to understand that there was a more historically established hierarchy in the Catholic Church.

In England as a child I had attended St Peter's School in York which is as old as the King's School, Canterbury, and was one of the oldest Anglican schools They were very traditional schools. But of late I have been quite aware that the Anglican Church had become very political in some quarters, very lax in attitudes regarding the admissions of gays to the ministry. I personally don't agree that gays should be ministers. I think this is anathema in Christianity though I personally have nothing against any, individually. I found that the Catholic Church had a clear, consistent teaching in this regard and this is also being shown in its attitude to gay adoptions. I cannot see how a child can be brought up in a fully nurturing way by two fathers or two mothers. A child needs a mother and a father.

In addition I found myself in agreement with the Catholic church's teaching on the ordination of women. This issue and that of gays entering ministry have biblical roots. It is strange that the Anglican Church cannot proclaim this but I think what has happened is that the Anglican Church has become politicised. I have found a stronger statement of the fundamental beliefs of Christianity in the Catholic Church, and it is a cause of wonder for me that the Church exists to this day. I really believe that the Catholic Church is the Church established by Christ, that it is stronger because of that. At the end of the day, there is not a great deal of difference between a traditional Anglican and traditional Catholic in the sense that the Masses are similar in both churches. I did not have a great knowledge of theology before the RCIA classes but I have learned a lot through them and so learned to appreciate the true meaning and beauty of the Mass as a Catholic understands it. The important thing is that I was never coerced as it was truly a personal decision to find out more and I don't regret it.

What about leaving your Anglican background?

Well in England all my family were Anglicans. They raised no difficulties regarding my conversion. Perhaps they wondered why I did it. Most reasonably committed Anglicans would not bother to change their religion – unless someone is particularly swayed by the facts and by the issue of women's ordination and the gay ministry issue (as we have seen in more recent times). It will be interesting to see where it all goes in the next 20 years.

How do you see the Anglicans now?

I must say I think Anglicans find it confusing that there are Wesleyans, Methodists and Uniting church groups among others. Why are there so many different denominations? Anglicans do not see themselves as a breakaway from the Church of Rome – they see themselves as a solid, consistent Christian entity. So "what's with the Uniting Church" one might say and "what's united about them and about many other Christian groups?" What about fringe groups like the Jehovah's Witnesses who claim bits and pieces of Christianity? In any town in England there may be an Anglican church, a Catholic church, perhaps a Uniting church. Protestants, I think, find it very confusing as to why there are other branches of Christianity in every part of England. I remember when I was in Oxford that there was a Lutheran church and I thought a bit about what they believed. The Orthodox seem a specific variant of Christianity in that they are geographically orientated – for example, the Greek Orthodox Church, the Russian Orthodox Church.

I know there are problems in all the churches these days, but within the Catholic Church one does not get some questionable, whacky branches or not as many as within the various Protestant groups, or so it seems to me. The Catholic community by comparison to me seems solid, simple and comparatively stable.

For me when I converted to the Catholic faith I felt I had found real certainties about the big questions at the centre of life. I am forever grateful for the people who helped me along the way in the parish of Coogee and to my lovely wife. The day I was baptised into the Catholic Church was a great day for me and I feel I am on a continuing journey of discovery and will be for the rest of my life.

15

Why I didn't convert to Eastern Orthodoxy: Fr Brian Harrison's story

Fr Brian Harrison OS was born in Sydney and from his earliest years pondered the spiritual realities. The following account gives an outline of Fr Harrison's thought as he delved deeply into what distinguished Catholicism from other Christian religions and what eventually led him to become a Catholic and a priest in the order of the Oblates of Wisdom. Fr Harrison is the author of several books on aspects of Catholicism and was emeritus professor of theology at the Pontifical Catholic University of Puerto Rico from 1989-2007. He continues to write on many aspects of Catholic theology and has given kind permission (as has Karl Keating of Catholic Answers Magazine*), to publish the following story of his conversion.*

I am probably a rather unusual convert to Catholicism, in that my spiritual journey to Rome involved both the other major world divisions of Christianity – Protestantism and Eastern Orthodoxy.[17] As an undergraduate university student, guided by the rational logos of classical philosophy (which Pope Benedict famously insisted upon as an attribute of God in his 2006 Regensburg discourse), I came to see the essential logical incoherence in Reformation Christianity: Its fundamental sola scriptura principle itself nowhere appears in Scripture and so is self-referentially contradictory.

I was also becoming increasingly convinced that if there is to be any true and definitive revelation from God to humanity, then

– given that God has plainly not decided to offer this revelation immediately and directly to each individual – he will need to establish a completely reliable intermediary, perennially accessible here on earth to ordinary people like you and me. In short, an infallible teaching authority. However, with further reading, I found myself confronted by the reality of two great communions – the two largest in Christendom, in fact – presenting themselves as rival claimants to the gift of infallibility. I had long known of the Catholic Church's claim to be the divinely appointed authority endowed with this charism. But now – in 1971, that is – I discovered the similar claim of Eastern Orthodoxy. Constantinople now flashed onto my radar screen as a challenger to Rome. How was I to decide between them?

Not quite "Catholic"

One reason for Orthodoxy's attractiveness back then was simply that, for me, its image remained refreshingly untainted by the emotional anti-Catholic Calvinist prejudices which I had imbibed against "Romanism" during adolescence. Nobody, as far as I knew, was describing Istanbul as "Mystery Babylon." I had read no reports of a Scarlet Woman, drunk with the blood of the saints, sitting astride a ten-headed Bosporus Beast. And I saw no accusatory fingers pointing at Constantinople's white-bearded patriarch as "that man of sin" – the Antichrist invading the temple of God and blasphemously speaking "great things" against the Lord and his elect.

However, after a couple of tentative Sunday visits to Greek Orthodox liturgies in Sydney (I am an Australian), after which I attempted to converse with the local priest, obstacles of a very different sort soon began to swing the balance back in the other direction. Given the priest's very limited knowledge of English, any serious discussion between us on doctrinal or theological matters proved to be impossible. Indeed, he seemed rather surprised that I, as an "Anglo," should even be interested in joining his denomination. All his other parishioners, even there in the centre of a large and cosmopolitan city, were ethnically Greek.

I was running up against the rather obvious fact that Orthodoxy is, well, not exactly catholic. It lacks the cultural universality and openness, the capacity to provide a true and welcoming home for all the world's tribes and nations, that is in fact one of the four marks of the true Church: one, holy, catholic, and apostolic. Every word of the liturgies I attended in Sydney – including the Scripture readings and preaching – was in Greek, of which I understood absolutely nothing. The thesis that Eastern Orthodoxy is the true religion was turning out to bear the practical corollary that, to share fully and fruitfully in the life of the Body of Christ, one would almost have to become a Greek. (Well, OK, maybe a Russian, a Serb, a Syrian – but in any case the ethnic options would be very limited.) And this sort of very burdensome de facto addition to the Gospel was plainly foreign to the New Testament. On the contrary, its message stresses that in Christ there is no longer Jew, Gentile, Greek.

Does Orthodoxy make sense?

In short, Eastern Orthodoxy, as far as I could see at that stage of my journey, had certain strengths over against Catholicism, but also certain weaknesses. So I still felt far from certain as to where to go. Indeed, I felt confronted by another version of the same problem I had faced earlier in trying to decide whether Protestantism was true or false: the problem of having to negotiate mountains of erudition that could easily occupy a lifetime of study, if I was to have any hope of arriving at a definitive answer. If these detailed questions of theology, exegesis, and history had kept the rival Catholic and

Orthodox experts in these fields interminably divided in spite of centuries of scholarly debate and oceans of spilled ink, who was I to presume the ability ever to reach any certainty as to which side was right? In this case the debate was mainly over the nature of the Petrine primacy, as revealed in Scripture and manifested in ancient church tradition. And that huge controversy looked very daunting – and the outcome very doubtful – for this not-very-erudite young amateur searching for a clear and certain answer.

Inevitably, in my prayers and studies, I began to wonder whether there was another quick, "silver bullet" argument like the one I had already found to be so fatal for Protestant theology? That is, could a clear answer perhaps appear from studying the internal logical coherence or incoherence of Orthodox claims, rather than from the attempt to accumulate, interpret, and evaluate endless masses of biblical and historical data? Eventually I found what I still believe to be that answer: I discovered a fatal flaw in Orthodoxy's account of how we can know what God has revealed. In what follows I shall use a series of several simple propositions to argue that Eastern Orthodoxy's account of how the Church transmits revelation is vitiated by a circular argument, and so cannot be true.

First, if God has given the gift of infallibility to his Church, there must be some identifiable authority or agent within her capable of exercising that gift. Now, Catholics believe that the College of Bishops – the successors of the apostles, led by the pope, the successor of St Peter – constitute that authority. The bishops can exercise the gift in several ways (as explained by Vatican Council II in article 25 of *Lumen Gentium*, the Dogmatic Constitution on the Church). The whole group (the College of Bishops) can teach infallibly, either gathered together in councils that its leader, the pope, recognises as "ecumenical" (that is, sufficiently representative of the whole Church), or even, under certain conditions, while remaining dispersed around the world. Finally, the pope, even when speaking alone, is guaranteed the charism of infallibility in his most formal (ex cathedra) pronouncements.

Now, what does the Eastern Orthodox communion see as the agent of the infallibility it claims for itself? In fact, it recognises only one of those forms of teaching mentioned above. Let us highlight this answer:

Proposition 1: Infallibility is to be recognised in the solemn doctrinal decisions of ecumenical councils.

However, does this mean that the Orthodox recognise the authority of all the same ecumenical councils that we Catholics recognise? Unfortunately not. While our separated Eastern brethren claim that, in principle, any ecumenical council between Pentecost and Judgment Day would enjoy the charism of being able to issue infallible dogmatic decrees, they recognise as ecumenical only the first seven councils: those that took place in the first Christian millennium, before the rupture between East and West. Indeed, even though they claim theirs is the true church, since that medieval split they have never attempted to convoke and celebrate any ecumenical council of their own. For they still recognise as a valid part of ancient tradition the role of the See of Peter as enjoying a certain primacy – at least of honour or precedence – over the other ancient centres of Christianity (Constantinople, Antioch, Jerusalem, and Alexandria).

Thus, mainstream Orthodox theologians, as I understand them, would say that for 1,000 years we have had a situation of interrupted infallibility. The interruption, they would maintain, has been caused above all by the "ambition", "intransigence" or " hubris" of the bishops of the See of Peter, who are said to have overstepped the due limits of the modest primacy bestowed on them by Jesus. However (it is said), once the Roman pontiffs come to recognise this grave error and renounce their claims to personal infallibility and universal jurisdiction over all Christians, why, then the deplorable schism will at last be healed! The whole Church, with due representation for both East and West, will once again be able to hold infallible ecumenical councils.

An insufficient proposal

This position, however, turns out to involve serious problems. Our separated Eastern brethren acknowledge that any truly ecumenical council will need to include not only their own representatives, but also those of the Bishop of Rome, whose confirmation of its decrees would in due course be needed, as it was in those first seven councils of antiquity. Well, so far so good. But does this mean the Orthodox acknowledge that the pope's confirmation of a council in which they participate will not only be necessary, but also sufficient, as a condition for them to recognise it as ecumenical? Unfortunately, the answer here is again in the negative. And it is the Easterners' own history which has, as we shall now see, reshaped their theology on this point during the last half-millennium.

After the East-West rupture that hardened as a result of the mutual excommunications of 1054 and the brutal sack of Constantinople by Latin crusaders in 1204, two ecumenical councils were convoked by Rome for the purpose of healing the breach. They were held at Lyons in 1274 and at Florence in 1439, with Eastern Christendom being duly represented at both councils by bishops and theologians sent from Constantinople. And in both cases these representatives ended up fully accepting, on behalf of the Eastern Church, the decrees, promulgated by these councils, that professed the true, divinely ordained jurisdiction of the successors of Peter over the universal Church of Christ – something much more than a mere primacy of honour. And these decrees were of course confirmed by the then-reigning popes.

Why, then, did neither of these two councils effectively put an end to the tragic and long-standing schism? Basically because the Eastern delegations to Lyons and Florence, upon returning to their own constituency, were unable to make the newly decreed union take practical effect. At Constantinople, the nerve-centre of the Byzantine Empire, an attitude of deep suspicion and even passionate hostility toward the Latin "enemies" was still strongly ingrained in the hearts and minds of many citizens – great and small alike. The result was that politics and public opinion trumped the conciliar agreements. The Eastern Christians as a whole simply refused to acquiesce in the idea of allowing that man – the widely feared and detested bishop of Rome – to hold any kind of real jurisdiction over their spiritual and ecclesiastical affairs.

As a result, in order to justify their continued separation from Rome, the Orthodox have had to nuance their position on the infallibility of ecumenical councils. They have had to maintain that the participation in a given council of bishops representing the whole Church and the confirmation of their decrees by the pope, while undoubtedly necessary, is still not sufficient to guarantee the true ecumenical status of that council. For over and above the fulfilment of those conditions, it is also necessary (so they have told us in recent centuries) for the faithful as a whole in both East and West – not just the pope and bishops or even the entire clergy – to accept that council's decrees as expressing the true faith. So the simple Proposition 1 set out above is now modified as follows:

Proposition 2: Infallibility is to be recognised in the solemn doctrinal decisions of those councils which are not only papally confirmed as ecumenical, but which are also subsequently accepted as such by the whole Church.

In the post-Enlightenment Western world, wherein opposition to clericalism (real or imagined), and the ideas of democracy and popular sovereignty have long enjoyed great popularity, this Eastern Orthodox ecclesiology, with its emphasis on the role of the laity, will naturally sound attractive to many. But on further examination a fatal logical flaw in the Orthodox theory comes to light.

Let's take a closer look here. If the crucial factor in deciding whether a given council's teaching is infallible or not depends on how it is received by the rank-and-file membership of "the whole Church", then it becomes critically important to know who, precisely, constitutes "the whole Church". How are her members to be identified? Who has voting rights, as it were, in this monumental communal decision?

A murky question of membership

In answer to this question, our Eastern friends cannot (and do not) say that for these purposes the whole Church consists of all who profess faith in Christ, or all the baptised. For on that basis the Orthodox would rule out as "un-ecumenical" (and thus, non-infallible) not only the second-millennium councils recognised by Rome and the Catholic Church, but also the seven great councils of the first millennium which they themselves recognise in common with Catholics! For each one of those councils was rejected by significant minorities of baptised persons (Arians, Monophysites, Nestorians, etc) who professed faith in Christ.

It is equally clear that the Orthodox cannot define the whole Church as Catholics do, namely, as consisting of all those Christians who are in communion with Rome, the See of Peter, the "Rock". For they themselves have not been in communion with Rome since medieval times. Could they perhaps try to define the whole Church in terms of communion with their own patriarchal See of Constantinople? No way. As far as I know, no Orthodox theologian has ever dared to claim that the need for union with Constantinople is part of revelation or divine law. For not only was this see itself in heresy at certain periods of antiquity, it did not even exist for several centuries after revelation was completed in the apostolic age.

In short, any Orthodox attempt to define the whole Church in terms of some empirically verifiable criterion will land our Eastern brethren in impossible absurdities. So the only other course open to them, logically, is the one they have now in fact adopted: They attempt to define the whole Church in terms of an empirically unverifiable criterion, namely, adherence to true, orthodox doctrine. Unlike cities, sayings, and sacraments, doctrinal orthodoxy cannot be recognised as such by any of the five senses. It cannot, as such, be seen, touched, or heard – only discerned in the mind and heart. Thus, if we ask the Orthodox why do they not recognise as constituent parts of the whole Church those baptised, Christ-professing Aryans, Nestorians, etc, who rejected one or more of the seven first-millennium councils, they will respond, "Why, because they were unorthodox, of course! They lapsed into heresy while we – and up till that time the Latin Church under Rome as well – maintained the true faith."

Now that the Orthodox position regarding infallibility and ecumenical councils has been further specified, we can reformulate it a third time, replacing the expression "the whole Church" at the end of Proposition 2 with another which clarifies what is meant by those three words:

Proposition 3: Infallibility is to be recognised in the solemn doctrinal decisions of those councils which are not only papally confirmed as ecumenical, but which are also subsequently accepted as such by the whole community of those Christians who adhere to true doctrine.

But here, I am afraid, we come face to face with the fundamental logical flaw in the whole Eastern Orthodox account of how we can know what – if anything – God has revealed to mankind. Since Christ founded his Church on earth to be a visible community, we cannot define her in terms of an invisible criterion – possession of doctrinal truth – without falling into absurdity. The flaw this involves is that of a circular argument – including the term to be defined within the definition itself. This results in a mere tautology: a repetitive proposition that provides no information at all.

We can see this more clearly if we remember that the whole purpose of an infallible church authority is simply to enable Christians to distinguish revealed truth clearly and certainly from falsehood and heresy. Keeping this in mind, we can formulate once again the Eastern Orthodox proposition, rewording Proposition 3 above so as to unpack the word infallible, spelling out its meaning and function.

Proposition 4: Christians can come to know with certainty *what is true doctrine* by recognising the solemn doctrinal decisions of those councils which are not only papally confirmed as ecumenical, but which are also subsequently accepted as such by the whole community of those Christians who *adhere to true doctrine*.

The words italicised above lay bare the underlying circularity – the tautology – that vitiates the logical coherence of Eastern Orthodox Christianity. We want to know how to identify true Christian doctrine with certainty, but the proffered solution to our problem assumes we already know the very thing we are seeking to discover. We are being told, "To discover what is true Christian doctrine, you must pay heed the teaching of those who adhere to true Christian doctrine"!

Not long after I came to the firm conclusion that Eastern Orthodoxy was illogical, so that its claim to infallibility could not be sustained, I was received into the Roman Catholic Church at the Mass of the Easter Vigil in 1972.

A problem at the root

It remains only to add that, over the years since I returned to full communion with the one Church founded by Christ, my conviction as a Catholic has only become stronger. For the Orthodox Church today is by no means in the same condition as it was then. The very features which had most attracted me to it back then have now largely faded into a twilight of doubt and confusion. For some centuries the tenacity of the Orthodox in adhering strictly to their ancient, stable liturgical traditions, together with their relative isolation from the post-Enlightenment West, combined to act as a quite powerful antidote, in practice, to the effects of the ingrained virus of illogicality that we have just exposed. But in recent decades, with more extensive cultural and ecumenical contacts, and with an increasingly large and active Eastern Diaspora in Western countries, Orthodoxy's underlying vulnerability to the same liberal and secularising tendencies in faith, morals, and worship that have devastated the West is becoming more apparent. That virus – an inevitable result of breaking communion with the visible rock of truth and unity constituted by the See of Peter – is now inexorably prodding Orthodoxy toward doctrinal pluralism and disintegration.

A traditionally minded Orthodox apologist might reply, of course, that confusion and dissent on these and many other matters are also rampant within Roman Catholicism, and indeed, to a great extent have spread to Orthodoxy as a result of powerful liberal and neo-modernist influences going largely unchecked in our own communion since Vatican Council II. This objection, unfortunately, is all too well founded as far as it goes. But it misses the vital point for present purposes, which is that the admittedly grave confusion in contemporary Catholicism is not due to its own underlying structure – its own fundamental theology of revelation. It is due rather to what many of us Catholics would see as a temporary weakness at the practical level: the level of Church discipline and government. We have witnessed a failure of many bishops, and arguably even recent popes, at times, to guard and enforce with sufficient resolve that doctrine which remains coherently and infallibly taught in theory and in principle by the Catholic magisterium. A solution to the present problems will not require the reversal of any Catholic doctrine; on the contrary, it will involve the more resolute insistence, in theory and in practice, on our existing doctrines. (This insistence, it is true, may need to include further authoritative papal interpretations of certain Vatican II texts whose ambiguity or lack of clarity betray something of the conflicting pastoral, philosophical, and theological tendencies that were apparent among the Council Fathers themselves.)

In Eastern Orthodoxy, on the other hand, the currently growing problem of internal confusion and division goes down to a deeper level. It is rooted in unsound principle, not just defective practice. It is a problem involving the essential defining feature of the Orthodox communion over against Catholicism, namely, its fateful medieval decision to repudiate the full primacy and authority of that rock established by Christ in the person of Peter and his successors in the See of Rome. Perhaps, if more of our Orthodox brethren can come to recognise the underlying logical flaw in their ecclesiology that I have tried to pinpoint and explain, we shall see more fruitful ecumenical progress toward the restoration of full communion.

16

Henry's conversion story

Henry Craft has lived in Canberra for most of his life and is retired after a long, successful career in public service. Here he recounts the questions that surfaced when he was a teenager attending school in Sydney where he lived as a child. One question led to another. Interestingly, a priest publicly evangelising in the Domain, Father Peter Little, took on Henry's questions and asked him several questions in return which resulted in several lively discussions. Here is Henry's story.

In 1966 I was 16 and a student at St Andrew's Cathedral School, an Anglican (Episcopalian) school. I would catch a bus into the city, crossing the Sydney Harbour Bridge. Although I barely noticed it, the bus passed St Patrick's Catholic Church, located in the inner city area and conducted by the Marist Fathers.

However, the church began to advertise a free lending library and, being a bookish young man, I started to borrow from the library. Later the parish advertised a series of talks on the Catholic Faith. The talks were given in a plain, factual manner and I did not find them particularly engaging. But one evening, the priest giving the talks asked what I thought of them. I made a polite, inconsequential response. And then he asked, did I think that I should convert to the Catholic Church. I was jolted from mere curiosity into actually considering the Catholic Church's claim to be the church that Christ had founded.

I began to read pamphlets published by the British Catholic Truth Society, which put the Catholic position clearly and cogently.

I began to think that the Protestant position, that the Bible alone is the authority for religious knowledge, was not a coherent basis for religious authority. I began to test this by arguing the point with a classmate, a staunch evangelical and the son of an Anglican clergyman. Presumably I failed to convince him as he later became a senior clergyman in the Anglican Church. For my part, I dismissed the Protestant position as untenable. But of course it was also necessary to consider whether the Catholic position on authority was itself coherent and indeed correct.

In those days, many people would go to the Domain, a public park in Sydney, on Sunday afternoons. There were speakers advocating various causes such as atheism, socialism and obscure mystical philosophies. A group would form around a speaker and often heckle in a determined but generally good natured manner. I had started visiting the Domain in my early teens and was entranced by its free flowing and sturdy debates.

At the edge of the Domain, about six middle aged men stood praying the rosary. They did not debate, and they remained silent when I once tried to interrogate them. Now, of course, I wonder whether I owe them the grace of my conversion. I will find out at the Final Judgement. Finding out how the prayers and merits of others have assisted in our salvation will surely be both a source of astonishment and great joy.

One Sunday afternoon, the late Father Peter Little SJ was speaking in the Domain. He faced persistent and vociferous heckling but consistently responded with a pleasant manner and logical answers. Then I raised my question: Could the Catholic Church argue for her authority from the Bible but criticise the Protestants who also regard the Bible as authoritative? Father Little explained that the Church argues initially from the New Testament as comprising historical documents and that, her authority being established, she then teaches that the Bible is in fact the inspired Word of God. His answer was coherent, and my subsequent musings have led me to accept it as veracious. My last problem with the Catholic position was removed.

Some people in the English tradition are concerned not to press things "too far" and even delight in maintaining positions that are splendidly eccentric. I considered this one afternoon as I walked home from school. Wouldn't it be rather romantic to continue as an Anglican while acknowledging the Pope as having some sort of primacy? And then I realised that God wanted me to become a Catholic and that I had no business resisting this. I can still point to the exact spot in the road where I came to this conclusion.

Although now committed to becoming a Catholic, I felt that I should seek an Anglican response and I approached my school's chaplain. He put forward one or two desultory arguments. Then he produced a Catholic liturgical text, quoting the *ipsissima verba* of the original Latin and arguing that this showed Catholics are idolaters. I knew nothing of the matter but suggested that perhaps the Latin might have different meanings in different contexts. The chaplain lost his temper saying this was a mere evasion. Our discussion came to an end but I felt I had discharged my duty to seek an Anglican response to the Catholic position.

About this time, a fleeting academic success led to me being interviewed on a local television station. When asked about my interests, I felt too embarrassed to say "Catholic doctrine" and instead professed an interest in "mediaeval theology". Happily, an apostolic Dominican, the late Father Reginald Batten, saw the programme. He wrote, urging me to study St Thomas Aquinas and inviting me to visit the priory where he was recuperating from a heart attack. As a result, I often visited him on Saturday afternoons. His wide-ranging and perceptive conversations helped form my Catholic outlook and helped me to commit to studying St Thomas.

I also discovered the Aquinas Academy, based at St Patrick's Church. It was directed by a Marist Father, the late Father Austin Woodbury, who had taken the then exceptional step of making Thomistic philosophy and theology available in the vernacular. However, as I was now in my matriculation year, I did not enrol in any units until the following year.

Although I had already realised that I should become a Catholic, discovering Thomism confirmed me in this decision. It is fashionable to dismiss the Thomistic tradition as unhelpful in the modern world, but I was exhilarated at discovering Catholic thinkers who were committed to pursuing a systematic and rigorous approach in religion.

The Thomist approach contrasted with an experience at the Sunday youth discussion group at St Andrew's Cathedral. The group was conducted by the Cathedral organist, a devout, friendly man, with postgraduate qualifications in music. One evening I gave a paper arguing that Christians should have some sort of Marian devotion. I was enchanted to have the convenor respond, "I agree with your premises and your logic is impeccable. But I can't accept your conclusion."

My parents were devout and committed Anglicans. When they realised that I had moved beyond a mere theoretical interest in Catholicism and now intended to leave the Anglican Church, they reacted strongly. They spoke of disowning me, and I formed romantic visions of myself as a victimised, homeless confessor of the Faith. In fact, I was not thrown out of home. They did burn my Catholic books and pamphlets, but it was too late – the ideas had taken root.

(Many years later, I visited my father about a week before his death. As I was leaving, I gave him a hug. He was very weak but astonished me by saying that he and my mother had been strongly opposed to my conversion but that he now respected my decision.)

My parents also arranged for me to meet several Anglican ministers. Reflecting on the points raised by the school chaplain and the other ministers, I noted that the Catholic position had a few central and powerful arguments about the source of religious authority, and that in contrast the Protestant position advanced many minor points. Some of these could be answered quickly but others might require more knowledge or thought. I concluded that a pressing and compelling argument addressing central issues should be preferred, and that a range of minor points that appear contrary should be regarded as problems to be resolved rather than as refutations.

I completed my schooling at the end of 1967 and was received into the Church on 3 February 1968, St Blaise's day.

Shortly afterwards, I began my university studies. I was fortunate that a full-time chaplain was available on the university campus. The late Father John King MSC celebrated Mass daily and encouraged students to study the Faith. His chaplaincy also acted as a social centre for a number of Catholic students, which was important for me as I did not have any other Catholic friends. By the way, I urge new converts to seek out Catholic friends: people of a similar age and background who believe and practise the Faith.

Looking back, it is likely that my conversion was a form of teenage rebellion but it was not *merely* teenage rebellion. Subconscious psychological factors do not remove the logical force of conscious thinking, which may in fact specify the specific kind of action that is adopted. For example, teenage rebellion might take the form of, say, becoming a Catholic, joining the Communist Party, or sexual misbehaviour. To put the matter another way, God works through the limitations of our imperfect psychologies.

In fact, my conversion is almost the only decision in my life about which I have no doubts or reservations. Accordingly, I will again express my gratitude to the priests who helped me along the way, while recognising that I have undoubtedly been helped by the prayers of others on earth and in heaven. But, above all, I give thanks to Almighty God for having brought me to His holy Church.

17

Conversion at the end of the journey

The following story is about a Sydney Catholic Bill Bradman and his friend Joe (not their real names). It describes a conversion which happened recently and the dramatic struggle that ensued between various people. Joe, like many others, had obstacles placed in the path of his interest in Catholicism. Bill tells how he came to be involved in Joe's conversion and what happened.

"My parents became communists and walked out on the Catholic Church. So when I was born in 1942, I was not baptised and not taught Christianity."

These were the first words of a 70-year-old Australian businessman sitting in my lounge room a few months back. So began an intriguing, very disappointing in some ways, but in the end, a very happy episode in my life.

The parish administrator in a suburb of a large Australian city asked me to give instructions in the Faith to an elderly and quite ill man of European birth. We will call him Joe Brunofski.

Joe was separated from his wife and had three adult children, two here in Australia and one living in Europe. He owned and ran a manufacturing business.

"About 12 months ago, it seemed that my recovery from prostate cancer was complete. I decided I would like to become a Christian. Of course, the question arose, what Christian denomination should I seek to join? My chosen method of research was to go to Sunday religious services of various denominations and then make a decision," Joe told me.

"The answer came faster than I expected. I went to Sunday Mass at a beachside Catholic Church. It was not like the other churches; the whole atmosphere was quite different. I really cannot describe it, but it appealed to me. My decision was made; I will try to join the Catholic Church," Joe said.

I told Joe that it would be a privilege to tell him about the Catholic religion. He took home with him my copy of *This Is the Faith* by Canon Francis Ripley.

Joe had someone very dear to him, his daughter Sally, living in Europe. They experienced a very special relationship. He was arranging to fly to Europe to see her. He didn't need to tell me that he had an inner compulsion to make this dash to the other side of the world to see Sally. He sensed, and he saw that I understood, that this would be the last time he would see Sally in this world.

Joe looked far too ill to make this long plane trip, but I knew that it would be cruel and insensitive for me to say this. So, I kept my mouth shut.

He did get to see Sally but was hospitalised for most of his time in Europe. On his return to Australia his condition was very serious. He immediately went into a Catholic hospital.

My surprises were about to begin.

I called the Catholic hospital and spoke with the senior Catholic Chaplain who was of course a priest. I explained to him that Joe was a very ill man but was seeking to become a Catholic and I politely requested him to visit Joe and to consider baptising him into the Church. His response stunned me: "Well Bill, that is much more problematic than you seem to realise. I have to be extremely careful; parish priests resent me cutting across their RCIA programmes. I can't just waltz in and baptise someone. This is a difficult and complex matter".

I had assumed – quite erroneously I was now starting to see – that all Catholic priests would love the opportunity to baptise a dying person and thereby probably ensure that person's eternal happiness. Clearly, this assumption was now being shaken.

Yet more surprises awaited me.

Joe left hospital for his suburban home. It is likely that doctors thought he would not live for very long.

I spoke with Joe on the phone and I had to be blunt and to the point. "Joe, I realise that you are very ill. The instructions in the Catholic Faith are not essential. If you wish, I can arrange a Catholic priest to visit you and you can be baptised into the Catholic Church."

Joe agreed immediately, but said that the priest would need to come when his carer was not present. I had previously spoken to his carer who came in between 10 am and 4 pm each weekday. She had made it very clear to me that she would block any communications between Joe and anyone from the Catholic Church.

I presented this situation to a parish priest in the suburb where Joe lived. He was pleasant but cautious about getting involved. "This is fraught with real difficulties and there are major privacy issues to consider," he told me.

I politely urged him to visit and baptise Joe and to move quickly as the man seemed to be approaching death. I thought, but didn't say, "Father this is really important. You are a Catholic priest and you can help this poor man to save his soul. Don't worry about the risks, just do what is critical: baptise Joe."

Subsequently, all attempts to make contact with this priest failed. My calls were always intercepted by a parish secretary who had a very laidback attitude towards Joe being baptised. Patronisingly, I was told that I was concerning myself too much about him. "Don't

Conversion at the end of the journey

worry about him as he will get baptism of desire; he doesn't need to be physically baptised," she told me.

Joe's health got worse. He was returned to the same Catholic hospital. Again, I spoke with the Catholic Chaplain but his attitude had not changed at all and I concluded that there was no way he would baptise Joe.

I talked with another priest whom I had known and respected for years. He was disgusted that the two priests mentioned had not gone ahead and baptised Joe. I explained to him that it looked as if my best option would be to baptise Joe myself.

He agreed and said that it would be easier for me than it would be for a priest to discreetly enter the hospital and baptise Joe. Being aware of all that had gone before, he advised me: "You will have to be clever. Get in there and baptise him, get out of the place and I suggest that you tell no one."

I drove to the hospital hoping to baptise Joe. More blocks awaited me. After a two hour wait, hospital staff advised me that Joe's daughter had instructed staff that her father receive no visitors. Since I refused to go away, the nurses eventually allowed me to speak with Joe's daughter.

I told her:

> Your father asked me to help him to become a Catholic. He said that he was born during World War II and that both his parents had renounced the Catholic Church and became communists. He said that he was not baptised and was never told anything about Christianity.

Joe's daughter was visibly very surprised and upset. She was not expecting this but allowed me to continue, although I sensed some hostility towards me:

> Your father told me that after going into remission from prostate cancer he decided to become Catholic. He visited

my local priest and that priest asked me to instruct him in the Catholic religion.

His daughter had heard enough and blurted out, "I had no idea he would do anything like that. I'm amazed. I am tempted not to believe you, but what you said about his parents giving up Christianity and becoming communists is true. That bit is absolutely correct."

Her hostility had grown rather than diminished. It was time to go. I wished her and her father well, gave her my phone numbers and asked her to let me know her father's condition. I did not expect her to call and she didn't.

I decided that I would drive to the hospital at 5.00 in the morning to baptise Joe. Good friend, Gary Goodwin, advised me to ask Our lady to take me by the hand and lead me to Joe.

I accepted his advice. Wandering around the hospital it was difficult to find Joe's ward. When I did find it, a lady was in the bed Joe had occupied. "Our Lady where are you taking me," I murmured to myself.

Joe had been moved to another building. Nursing staff were having a smoke at the basement entrance. They happily used their computer card to give me entrance. I sailed through the next checkpoints.

Amazingly, the duty nurse outside Joe's room seemed to know exactly what was going on, without my telling her anything. She said, "I will take you to Joe but you will have to be quick because his family will arrive very soon and you will need to be gone by then." Clearly, Our Lady was making the path very smooth for me now.

Joe was nearing the end and our conversation was brief. He agreed to be baptised. Taking water from my pocket, I baptised him. I had never previously given this sacrament. For Joe, in a sense, it should have occurred 70 years earlier, at the start of his earthly pilgrimage, and not right at the end.

The Good Thief on Calvary grabbed salvation with his last breath and Our Blessed Lord promised him, "This day you will be with me in paradise." What a beautiful event that was. I thought Joe's baptism was similar in a certain respect and thanked God for the unforgettable opportunity to be His instrument.

It is most unlikely that Joe saw a Catholic priest after his baptism. Even if there had been a priest seeking to comfort and pray with him, his family would have had roadblocks in place.

In two more days Joe was dead, but no one from his family or the hospital rang to tell me. The records of this big Catholic hospital will never show he died a Catholic, but indeed he did. Virtually no one in this world knows that he won the great treasure of joining the Catholic Church in the last moments of his earthly life. If the family write a family history, this beautiful, final turn in his life will not rate a mention.

He was given a Protestant funeral service which I attended. After the service, his daughter, who had stopped me from seeing her father, spotted me and gave me a withering stare. So, I left for home. It doesn't really matter, but some intriguing questions will have to remain unanswered: Why was she so vehemently opposed to her father achieving his dying wish to become Catholic? Will she ever know, in this world, why I persisted in my attempts to baptise him and that it is likely he is happy in heaven today and praying for her happiness?

Perhaps there is nothing in my experience that my friends have found as interesting and even stunning as this event. Some have asked, what does event mean to me? So, here is my answer: God chose me to do an important job. I was not the best qualified for it, but he gave it to me and, it seems, and to no one else. Perhaps, from all eternity God saw Joe seeking salvation right at the end of his life and He offered an unlikely layman the grace to take up the challenge to be an instrument in Joe's salvation.

It is with humility, I hope, that I can add. God chose me to baptise Joe so that all his sins and the punishment due to sin would be wiped away. And, as a consequence, on his death he would encounter Jesus Christ and enter the unending happiness of heaven.

In my wallet, I have a list of 20 plus canonised saints to whom I pray every day. Joe Brunofski is now on that list. It is unlikely that he will ever be canonised but I am confident that he is a saint in heaven and I am counting on him to intercede for me.

... AND SOME MORE CONVERSION STORIES FROM ALL OVER

18

Ex-communist becomes a Catholic

Galina lives in Moscow and works for the Catholic Church as a pro-life advocate and public speaker. She was once a communist and personally recounted her story to me when we met in 1999 at an HLI conference in Canada and later when I went to meet her in 2005 in Moscow. The following recounts a tumultuous journey from her communist roots to the long path of questioning that led her to become a Catholic. She heard just one thing about Jesus Christ in her youth – that he was a "dangerous man" and to be avoided at all costs.

Galina Maslennikova, a psychologist living in Moscow, was once head of a Youth Komsomol Brigade, the communist organisation for youth. Strange as it may be to read the following, this former atheist and communist is now is a pro-life Catholic, heads a Russian Family Life Centre and has prayed outside abortion clinics in Moscow. Galina's journey, contemporary and dramatic, is worth recounting as an example that even in the darkness of our age, amidst the devastating legacy of the communist regime, God uses little ones as his helpers and instruments in the unfolding of his plans. Galina is the Russian way of saying "Helen" – and on this principle Hollywood is "gollywood". Galina is a living example of the extraordinary and surprising power of God and here follows her story as I recall it.

I first met Galina over a decade ago at a pro-life conference. We were accidentally billeted to the same room in the conference hotel. She related her story to me at this 1999 Human Life International Conference (HLI) which was held in Toronto from 7-11 March of that year. She was attending her first pro-life conference ever and on her first trip outside Russia. Galina herself, a slightly built, softly spoken woman in her 50s, with searching eyes, walked through the door of the hotel room we were to share, with just a handbag. She told me the airline had lost her suitcases (this on her first trip to the West!) and all she had were the clothes she stood in and her handbag. She spoke in Polish, which was really fortunate, as I happen to speak the language having Polish ancestors on my father's side. I asked Galina if she had had something to eat and she told me she did not need to "eat today" as she had "eaten yesterday". She had had a long journey and waits in airports. Her eyes had a look in them that seemed to say, "We do not live by bread alone," and she quite contentedly put down her handbag. From this little encounter I began to get the sense that here was an unusual person, a deep thinker who lived in another realm. Bit by bit I found out about the life she led.

First, she told me how she got to Toronto and what had happened. She had been sent a ticket by HLI's Polish office in Gdansk and having no idea what to expect, flew out to the "West" on a wing and a prayer and a light suitcase. She had no money; just the ticket. This may not seem remarkable in itself but all things considered, it is nothing short of a miracle that she arrived in Toronto at that time. She was picked up from the airport and arrived virtually penniless in a new destination, being too shy to ask for any more than she had been given and had not even enough money to buy what many of us take for granted, a cup of coffee while waiting for a plane. As things turned out, during the first leg of her journey her suitcase got lost en route and then was found soon afterwards. Galina was duly compensated US$100 for the inconvenience by the airline. Then it happened a second time on the second leg of her journey to Toronto when I met her without her luggage. Galina was compensated a second time for the lost, then found suitcase with another US$100.

I saw the lost suitcase delivered to the door of the hotel in Toronto. So within one day of being in the West, she was carrying $200 in her pockets and saying prayers of thanksgiving. God had taken care of her needs in a simple, outstanding way.

However, this is only one slender detail of a remarkable story. Over the period of the conference, many came to know something of Galina's life and of her journey from atheism to Catholicism. She had grown up in the thick of the Soviet Union and was looking wide-eyed at the "free West". In fact, it was more than a little ironic that one of the first things I had to explain to her was the presence of Canadian Mounted Guards near the hotel where the conference participants were staying. The famed police on horses called the Mounties were there to prevent disruptions of the conference by protesters who wanted to verbally assault pro-lifers at every opportunity. They stood around the hotel chanting vociferously, the text of their placards, "Pro sex, pro gay, pro abortion all the way". Thinking she could not leave the hotel without permission from the "authorities", I told Galina breezily that this was "the West" and she was allowed to go wherever she wanted; but in reality it was wisest to stay put for a few hours until the protest was over. In fact, the Canadian Mounties were preventing anyone from entering or leaving the hotel. It is amazing that Galina's first experience was the curtailment of free movement in the West due to the politically correct and loud protests outside the hotel. She needed to be protected from violence, as did we all. It was a strange introduction to life in the "free West" and the virulent nature of anti-life protests. But the time that we were holed up in the hotel gave us a chance to speak and so I learned of the journey that brought her from communism to being a Catholic and indeed pro-lifer.

How it all began

Galina was born in Tashkent in Uzbekistan in an atheist family. She was of Russian background but lived in Uzbekistan because Russians were often sent to various other parts of the Soviet empire to work. She lost both parents to illness at the age of 14 and then lived with an older sister, joining the communist Youth organisation, Komsomol. She, like her Russian confreres, learned the principles of communism well and was always warned about not having anything to do with Christians. She recalls being told in one session that Jesus Christ was a dangerous person and she was to have nothing to do with him. She admits in retrospect, that she wondered at the time why such emphasis was put on avoiding Christ but when she asked innocently, no-one could give her a straight answer. After an earthquake in 1966 which damaged Tashkent, Galina and her sister moved to Tomsk in Russia where she studied at the University there. After completing her degree she was sent to work in Lwiw in the Ukraine (formerly *Lwów* in Poland). As previously stated, many Russians were sent to work in various parts of the former Soviet Union and many non-Russians were sent all over Russia. It is quite fortuitous that she was sent to a country, where there was not only a strong Orthodox tradition but also a Catholic tradition – the Ukrainian Catholics are called Uniates or Greek Catholics. They were previously Orthodox and reunited with Rome in the 16th century by means of the Union of Brest-Litovsk in 1596. They have existed side by side with the Orthodox for several centuries. But Galina knew nothing of that – she just moved to Lwiw to start her new job.

Walking past a church in *Lwów*

One day during the late 1980s in Lwiw, Galina found herself walking along the street past a large Ukrainian Catholic church with open doors. As she walked she looked sideways at the open door and some curiosity drew her to this place which she heard talked about – which was established by the "dangerous" person Jesus Christ. Something induced her to enter and as she did so – she always remembers this moment – for the first time she felt a strange peace she had not experienced before. She simply could not account for this feeling and just sat at the back of the church staring at the sanctuary not knowing the meaning of anything before her. She recalls gazing at the tabernacle and sensing something very strange, very tranquil and ultimately very inviting, as if someone were there. She could put no concept, no thought, no word on this experience – she simply gave herself to it and then walked out again pondering what had happened to her.

This was the first of regular trips to the church over the next year. She says at that time she did not pray as she did not know how. She did not talk to anyone in the church and no-one approached her. It is difficult for Westerners to understand that in the communist era (this was just prior to the end of the Soviet Empire), churchgoers were afraid of spies reporting on them. If people went to church at all, they went quietly and prayed together but without too much social exchange, unless they knew for certain that the person to whom they spoke could be trusted. Priests could never be sure that there was not a spy sitting in the pews ready to report them at the first opportunity. One priest in Poland had been arrested not long before for explaining that abortion was wrong, as this was contrary to Soviet policy. People in churches had a healthy, perhaps at times unhealthy suspicion, and so only spoke to trusted friends and even then they said little.

So there was Galina, month after month, sitting at the back of the church hearing about God, Christ and "The Holy Spirit". She heard that there was a place called heaven, another called hell, someone called "the Blessed Virgin", Joseph, saints and a book called the

Bible but still she could not piece this mysterious plot together. What did it all mean? For it seemed a most interesting story to her even though some bits did not seem to hang together. Who really was Saint Joseph?

One day Galina approached a member of the congregation of the church she frequented and asked, without too much ado, where she could get a copy of the book called "The Bible". Fortunately, the mistrust inherent in a situation like this melted away. Perhaps the congregation had figured out by this time that Galina was not a spy or perhaps they saw the yearning in her eyes. She was told she would be given a copy of this book in Russian the following week. Galina was thrilled to receive the Bible and went home eagerly to piece the story together. Cradle Catholics might imagine the drama of encountering the story of God's love and mercy for the first time and how differently life must have looked to Galina in those hours at night spent poring over the pages of this new-found treasured book. Galina did in fact read enough to decide finally that she would try to join these "Christians", believing that they had the right take on reality.

Meanwhile Galina's two teenage daughters, who lived with her, had become suspicious of her sorties and had even tried to follow her. Suspicion mounted on suspicion and they eventually questioned her about where she went in her time off. Then they heard about these trips to "a church" and had discussed with each other what this could all possibly mean, genuinely concerned for their mother's wellbeing. This was a spiritual journey which had whiffs of espionage about it. However, rather than being put off by their mother's clandestine activities, they were increasingly fascinated by them and ended up being drawn into the mysterious journey she was on. They confronted their mother with the results of their observations and she told them that she was searching for the truths of Christianity. They were shocked, puzzled yet fascinated at what she was up to.

Galina decided it was time to convert. Not knowing of any differences between Eastern Orthodox and Uniate Catholics in the Ukraine, Galina made some phone calls, and as things turned out, ended up contacting the Orthodox office in that town and was directed to come in and see an Orthodox priest. She went, heart thumping, with a friend to give moral support, not knowing what to expect. She found herself in a crowded waiting room of an Orthodox priest's house. She says she was scared and held both hands together as she was shaking so much with fear as she waited for her turn to have an interview.

Suddenly an elderly lady, hardly able to walk, slowly opened the door to the waiting room and limped inside. She had appeared out of nowhere it seemed and approached Galina, asking her distinctly where the Catholic church was. Galina knew that the church she had been going to up till now was called "Catholic", without knowing what this word meant. Having pity on the old lady, her friend suggested that they should take the old lady there to her destination as she looked too frail to make it by herself. Galina agreed and cancelled the appointment for now. So the two women left the Orthodox church office, helping the elderly lady catch a bus to the Catholic church for which she had asked directions, and took her up to the church door. As they arrived together, the lady went inside and Galina found herself in the presence of a Catholic priest who had walked outside at that precise moment. Galina then thought she may as well reveal her plans to this priest as to anyone else, as she might not get another chance. So she told him she wanted to be a Christian, upon which the priest replied, "The Holy Spirit has led you here." It was a moment as dramatic as if the prophet Elijah himself had appeared right there and then, or as if it were an event in a Dostoyevsky novel. The course of Galina's life was changed forever and from that moment on, Galina says, she felt a strong inner conviction that she was meant to be there and trusted the priest who signed her up for six months instruction.

As events turned out, Galina's daughters, who had been so suspicious of their mother's activities, followed her journey and in the end they all became Catholics in a triple Baptism on 6 January 1989, St Nicholas' day. The priest predicted Galina would take the faith to others, which surprised her immensely. In fact Galina has shown that she could touch people's lives profoundly doing her best to spread the Gospels in what was to be soon post-revolutionary Russia – from St Petersburg to Lake Baikal.

Galina goes to an abortion clinic to pray ...

Galina relates, in the course of her dramatic story, that after her conversion she became aware of the culture of death – the hopelessness particularly expressed in the extent of abortion in her country and the world. She felt moved to help the young girls who felt they had no hope, no meaning in life, no alternative but to go to abortion clinics. She went to pray outside an abortion centre in Moscow and offered alternative advice to girls on their way to the clinic. It is a tragic feature of this extraordinary country that Russia has long had one of the highest abortion rates in the world and whatever the political persuasion of any given demographers, all agree the country now faces a serious demographic decline, as does much of western Europe as well. Galina, like Gideon of old, went to confront the abortion Goliath with simplicity, prayer and unbounded trust in God. And her prayers resulted in many turnarounds.

Galina has the gift of transmitting hope and trust and the young girls listened to her. She related that once she spoke with a young girl outside the Moscow clinic where she prayed. The girl had been told that the child she was carrying was disabled and had been advised that an abortion would "be best" for her. Galina suggested the girl take time to talk to her and the girl accepted the invitation to see the Russian version of the video *The Silent Scream*, which centres around Dr Bernard Nathanson's account of what occurs in an abortion. While watching it, she had a change of heart saying "I don't care if my child is disabled – this is a child, my child who should not be harmed." As things turned out she had a perfectly normal child and soon afterwards was married to a nice man who also converted to Catholicism and loved her and her child. The girl is forever grateful that she met Galina on the street. I asked Galina if she had ever heard of the Helpers of God's Precious Infants, whose peaceful presence outside clinics has changed many women's minds in a similar way. She said she'd never heard of them and I informed her that she in fact was doing what this network of pro-life prayer and practical help was doing around the world each day.

In fact, now some decades afterwards, Galina has a string of conversions behind her and in an ironic twist, she moves the hearts of people in the West by the strength of her faith. Her intense constant awareness of the spiritual realities is not only Dostoyevskean, it is "First century Israel' – she is like a living flame going from town to town from Irkutsk to St Petersburg, from Moscow to Riga, witnessing to the depth of the spirit in her every action and word. Her whole life radiates a quality of someone who is totally immersed in the mercy of God and who cannot keep from telling others of it.

As if what has already been related of Galina's life is not already remarkable enough, she related to me another fascinating fact, this time about her family history. One day towards the end of our stay, she showed me a hundred-year-old rosary. Many generations ago someone in her Russian family had married a Polish Catholic and the rosary was a puzzling heirloom passed down through the generations of her family. As Galina's family were all atheists, no-one really knew quite what to do with it, though they did not want to discard it. An aunt who was one of the most recent inheritors of the rosary thought that Galina might like to have it and so she gave it to her. Galina realised that four to five generations ago, someone in her family used these beads and prayed rosaries that had been, and always would be, a continual source of grace for her, her family and for her entire country.

19

On converting from Buddhism to Catholicism: one convert's story

Paul Williams is a Catholic convert from Buddhism, lay Dominican, and professor at the University of Bristol (UK). He is married and has three grown children. He is Professor of Indian and Tibetan Philosophy at the University of Bristol. He sees his journey as one of leading to authentic hope. Here is his story.

I am a Catholic, a convert. Indeed I am now a lay member of the Dominican Order. But I was a Buddhist for over 20 years, and what I want to concentrate on here is Buddhism and rebirth. In talking about Buddhism and rebirth, I shall really be telling you a little about my own conversion story, a conversion story that is of course one of change, wonderful welcome change, and I shall argue it was a change from very real hope-lessness to hope.[18]

My journey to Buddhism

I wasn't always a Buddhist. As far as I recall our immediate family was not particularly religious, although on our father's side there were practising Anglicans and relatives had been Anglican vicars. On our mother's side I do not remember any especial interest in religion. I heard once that our maternal grandmother had said she would be a Buddhist if she were anything at all. I discovered fairly recently that in fact our maternal grandfather's family was traditionally Catholic, although he had abandoned the faith. I am not sure now why, but for some reason when I was really quite young I joined the local Anglican church choir. I loved singing church music. Unfortunately my voice broke rather early and, since I was thought to be too young to be a bass, as far as I recall I spent my entire time as Head Chorister miming. This perhaps gave me an early taste of the bluff necessary for an academic career.

At the appropriate age early in the 1960s I was confirmed in the Anglican Church by the Bishop of Dover. I became a server at Holy Communion. As the '60s wore on I became involved in the lifestyle and all the normal things that teenage boys get up to. As public examinations loomed larger, I left the choir, ceased to be a server, and lost contact with the Church. I grew long hair, and dressed strangely.

I went to the University of Sussex to read philosophy. By that time, in common with many in the late 1960s, I had developed an interest in meditation and things Indian. I channelled this interest particularly into Indian philosophy. I subsequently took my doctorate in Buddhist philosophy at the University of Oxford.

By about 1973-ish I was already beginning to think of myself as a Buddhist. I finally "Took Refuge", formally becoming a Buddhist, in the Dalai Lama's tradition of Tibetan Buddhism. When I found myself teaching at the University of Bristol in the early 1980s I set up with others a group in Bristol that also now has its own Buddhist Centre. I became involved in occasional teaching within the context of practising Buddhism at Buddhist Centres. As well as my academic work in Buddhist philosophy I wrote and spoke as a Tibetan Buddhist on television, the radio, and at conferences. I took part in public and private dialogue with Christians, including Hans Küng and Raimundo Pannikkar.

I was interested in philosophy, but also in meditation and the exotic East. Many of us found Buddhism attractive originally because among other things it seemed so much more rational than the alternatives (but also much, much more exotic). In particular

Buddhism seemed much more sensible (and exotic) than a theistic religion like Christianity. Buddhists do not believe in God. Well, (we thought) there seemed no reason to believe in God, and the existence of evil presented for us a positive argument against the existence of God. Those of us who were brought up as Christians were fed up with defending the existence of God in an unsympathetic world against its detractors. When we stood back and tried to be as objective as possible God looked less and less likely. In Buddhism one has an immensely sophisticated (and exotic) system of morality, spirituality and philosophy which does not require God at all. At a stroke difficulties involved in accepting the existence of God were bypassed. Instead, in becoming a Buddhist, (we thought) one could be a meditator with Buddhists, the ones who really know about meditation.

Rebirth

However, over many, many years as a Buddhist I became more and more uneasy about my Buddhism. Absolutely central to my growing unease with Buddhist affiliation were worries about rebirth and associated worries about the doctrine of karma. Buddhists believe in rebirth, that is, as it is broadly understood, reincarnation. And, Buddhists claim, there is no chronological first beginning to the series of past lives. We have all of us been reborn an infinite number of times. No God is needed to start the series off – for there simply was no first beginning. Things have been around (somewhere) for all eternity.

Now, belief in rebirth (and indeed karma – I'll come that) seems to be quite common nowadays even among those who would not claim to be Buddhists or Hindus. One even finds Christians who say they believe in rebirth. But rebirth was well-known in ancient Greece and Rome, and it has never been part of Christian orthodoxy. And there are good reasons for this. Rebirth is incompatible with certain absolutely central Christian doctrines, including the inestimable value of each and every individual person, and the justice of God. If rebirth is true, realistically we really have no hope. It is a hopeless doctrine. As a Buddhist, it dawned on me that I had no hope. Let me explain.

Hands up who wants to be reborn as a cockroach?

I want you to imagine that you are told you are to be painlessly executed at dawn. You are terrified. You are not terrified because it will hurt, since it will be painless. So why are you terrified? Perhaps your fear lies in it being the end of all your projects for the future – the story is over. Or maybe you do not want to leave forever your friends and family. Or perhaps you fear just a great empty void, a nothingness. What is it, exactly, that frightens you?

Now I want you to imagine that your executioner gently puts his arm round you and tells you not to worry. It really isn't so bad. Although you are to be executed, it has been discovered without a shadow of a doubt that the Buddhists and Hindus were right after all. You are to be instantly reborn. In fact, you are to be reborn as a cockroach in South America.

Well – I suggest that you would still be terrified. Indeed you might be even more frightened. But why would you be so frightened? Being a cockroach answers all, or most, of the fears that first sprang to mind when you heard of your imminent execution. Cockroaches surely have projects for the future, to get enough food, poison humans, or whatever it is cockroaches happily spend their lives doing. It'll be fun, once you get used to it. Of course, being a cockroach still means you must leave your friends and family, but then in life we often leave our friends and family. Our family and friends may be separated from us by exile, war, quarrels or whatever. Or if they die, instead of you, it has the same effect. So why in this respect should we be more terrified of our own death, than of the deaths of our loved ones? Moreover as a cockroach you will have lots and lots of new friends and family, many, many cockroach friends and cockroach family to replace the ones you have lost. You'll get used to it. It's not so bad, not half as bad as you thought. And being a cockroach is not nothingness. It's not like a great empty void. It is a life, too. You will still live.

So why are we not consoled by all this? Why do we still not relish the idea of execution at dawn, followed by all the fun of being a cockroach in South America? Well, you might say, cockroaches are horrible, ugly, verminous creatures. Who wants to be one? But is that fair? Perhaps cockroaches are not horrible and ugly to themselves. After all, I expect their mummies love them.

Can you imagine being a cockroach? Can you imagine living that cockroachy life? Surely you cannot. We are not asking can you imagine waking up inside a cockroach's body (as Kafka tells us, in his story Metamorphosis). We are not asking you to imagine being you, somehow having to come to terms with being crammed inside a cockroach's body. That would not be much fun. You would have problems with all those legs, at least for a while, and you would hate your cockroach mummy getting anywhere near you. She is so creepy! But it wouldn't be like that, would it? You would love your cockroach mummy, because (I expect) cockroaches do love their mummies. For you would be a cockroach too. You cannot imagine what it would be like to be a cockroach, because you would not be you inside a cockroach body. You would be a cockroach. And who knows what the imaginations, the dreams, of a cockroach might be.

Rebirth means the end of me

What is my point here? My point is this: What is so terrifying about my being executed at dawn and reborn as a cockroach is that it is simply, quite straightforwardly, the end of me. I cannot imagine being reborn as a cockroach because there is nothing to imagine. I quite simply would not be there at all. If rebirth is true, neither I nor any of my loved ones survive death. With rebirth, for me – the actual person I am – the story really is over. There may be another being living its life in some sort of causal connection with the life that was me (influenced by my karma), but for me there is no more. That is it – end of it. There is no more to be said about me.

None of this in itself means the Buddhist position is wrong. But what it does mean is that, if the Buddhist position is correct, our death in this life is actually, really, the death of us. Death will be the end for us. Traditionally, at least on the day to day level, Buddhists and others who accept rebirth tend to obscure this fact in their choice of language by referring to "my rebirth", and "concern for one's future lives". But actually any rebirth (say, as a cockroach in South America) would not be oneself, and there is a serious question therefore as to why one should care at all about "one's" future rebirths.

I began to see that if Buddhism were correct then unless I attained enlightenment (nirvana) or something like it in this life, where the whole cycle of rebirth would finally come to a complete end, I would have no hope. Clearly, I was not going to attain enlightenment in this life. All Buddhists would be inclined to accept that as true concerning just about everyone. Enlightenment is a supreme and extremely rare achievement for spiritual heroes, not the likes of us – certainly not the likes of me. So I (and all my friends and family) have in themselves no hope. Not only that. Actually from a Buddhist perspective in the scale of infinite time the significance of each of us as such, as the person we are, converges on nothing. For each of us lives our life and perishes. Each one of us – the person we are – is lost forever. Buddhism for me was hope-less. But was I absolutely sure Buddhism was true? As St Paul knew so well, Christianity at least offers hope.

Karma

Let me say something now about the theory that usually goes along with that of rebirth, the theory of karma. This is the theory, broadly, that our virtuous and vicious actions have respectively pleasant and painful results for us. Thus if I stub and break my little toe, that painful experience is as such the result of a vicious deed done by me in the past. If what I have said so far is correct then the principles of karma when applied over lifetimes must mean that some persons escape altogether at least some of the results of their vicious deeds, and others receive unpleasant experiences that result from vicious deeds they did not do.

For consider the following: Supposing a horrible dictator gives orders on his deathbed for painfully executing a thousand people. That dictator dies, so that person – the dictator – never receives the nasty results due to him through karma. There no doubt will be another being, "his rebirth" who will receive those horrible results. But, first, what is that to our dictator? And, second, clearly that other being (the rebirth) will be horribly hurt as a result of something he, she, or it, did not do. The idea that a baby, for example, suffers from a painful illness because of something another person did, even if the baby is in some sense a rebirth of that person, can scarcely be portrayed as satisfactory or just. It could certainly not be, as some have claimed, the most acceptable answer to the problem of evil. The baby simply is not that person who did the wicked deed, no more than a baby cockroach is me after my execution.

Buddhists do not hold that God exists, but if there were a God certainly the theory of karma would be quite incompatible with His justice. So, too, would be the throwing away of persons on the rubbish heap of history which is entailed by rebirth.

The Christian has hope

It seems to me patently obvious that if I am reborn the person I am now in this life ceases to exist. This is blindingly obvious if I am reborn as a cockroach in South America. We could not say that I am the same person as a cockroach in South America. Could we any more say I would be the same person if my rebirth involved a human embryo in Africa? Or in Bristol, in my own family? And the standard Buddhist position (correctly) explicitly denies that the rebirth is the same person as the one who died. Thus rebirth is incompatible with the infinite value of the person.

But Christianity is the religion of the infinite value of the person. The person we are, or can become, is not accidental to us, and is not unimportant. Each person is an individual creation of God, as such infinitely loved and valued by God. On this is based the whole of Christian morality, from the value of the family to the altruism and self-denial of the saints. Because we are infinitely valuable to God Jesus died to save each one of us. He did not die to save chains of rebirths, or reincarnating selves. He died to save us. And we are the persons we are, as embodied individuals with our stories, families and friends. Contrary to the myth of the Christian hatred of the physical and the body, actually Christianity is also the religion of embodiment and the essential goodness of all physical creation.

It follows from all this that rebirth would be diametrically opposed to the whole direction of Christianity. If there is survival of death – and the faith of the Christian, originating in Christ's own resurrection, is based on that – it cannot be in terms of rebirth.

Rebirth and the infinite value of the person are incompatible. The Christian view of death is one of hope, indeed of triumph, for (apart from anything else) it sees death not as an empty void, a nothingness. The story is not over for the persons we are, and we can hope that we do not part forever from our friends and family. But much, much more, our faith is that in God our deaths will be meaningful for each and every one of us – each individual person – in ways that exceed our imaginations but that even now excite our hope and draw-on our lives.

Conclusion

Well – it was thoughts like this that gradually led me away from Buddhism. Buddhism was for me hope-less. Christians have hope. I so wanted to be able to be a Christian. I returned, to look again at the things that I had rejected in my earlier Christian faith. I detail the stages of my journey in my book *The Unexpected Way* (T&T Clark/ Continuum: 2002). Through grace I came again to God. I convinced myself that it was rational to believe in God, as rational – indeed I now think more rational – than to believe with the Buddhists that there is no God. Coming to believe in God, I could no longer be a Buddhist. I had to be a theist. I looked carefully at the evidence and was astonished to find that the literal resurrection of Our Lord from the dead after His crucifixion was the most rational explanation of what must have happened. That, I felt, made Christianity the most rational option out of theistic religions. And, as a Christian, I argued that priority has to be given to the Catholic Church. I needed a good reason not to be received into that Church. In my book I examine various arguments that were given to me against becoming a Catholic, and I argue that as a reason for rejecting the Catholic Church they fail to convince. So I was received into the Catholic Church.

I now live in gratitude and hope. And I have never, ever, for one moment regretted my decision.

Addendum

If what I have argued here is correct, then it seems to me we are entitled theologically to say that we know rebirth is false. What I mean by this is:

   i) Rebirth is incompatible with Christian belief.

   ii) As Christian believers we are entitled to say that we know theologically that Christian belief is true.

   iii) Whatever is incompatible with a truth is false.

   iv) Hence we are entitled to say as Christian believers that we know theologically that rebirth is false.[19]

20

From abortion advocate to Catholic

All the conversion stories within this volume are dramatic but perhaps Bernard Nathanson has become the modern day equivalent of a St Paul, not in the immediacy of his conversion, but in the extent of the dramatic turnaround he has made. Bernard Nathanson was the president of NARAL (National Association for the Repeal of Abortion Laws) in the 1970s, and as such, was one of the foremost proponents of abortion's pro choice movement. Nathanson fought for the legalisation of abortion at the time of the Roe vs Wade *decision in the years leading up to the overturn on the abortion ban in 1973. His conversion was from a very dark place of loneliness and desolation from which he was led by a desire to see if anything existed beyond his way of seeing things. In a story revealing much anguish, the following account tells how he came to consider the truths Christ revealed to the world and in a way that continued to amaze not only those who followed his journey but also, one suspects, Nathanson himself.*

Bernard Nathanson was born in New York City into a Jewish family, though he abandoned his Jewish faith in his youth and later referred to himself as a "Jewish atheist" or more simply an atheist. His father was an obstetrician/gynaecologist, the same career that Nathanson pursued in his professional life. He graduated in 1949 from the McGill University Faculty of Medicine in Montreal, was licensed to practise in New York state in 1952 and became board-certified in obstetrics and gynaecology in 1960.

Nathanson fought the pro-life movement with great gusto and

determination. So involved was he in the push to legalise abortion in the United States, he even admitted to fabricating polls saying Americans supported abortion. As one of the founding members of NARAL (National Association for the Repeal of Abortion Laws), Nathanson later described the lies he and his fellow abortion proponents devised to push the legalisation of abortion. These included fabricating polls saying Americans supported abortion as well as illegal abortion statistics. On a website explaining this fabrication, Nathanson says that the "actual figure (of illegal abortions) was approaching 100,000, but the figure we gave to the media repeatedly was 1,000,000".[20] The same account reports Nathanson saying, "I remember laughing when we made those slogans up", as he reminisces about the early days of the pro-abortion movement in the late '60s and early '70s. He also states that he was "looking for some sexy, catchy slogans to capture public opinion. They were very cynical slogans then, just as all of these slogans today are very, very cynical". He adds, "Repeating the big lie often enough convinces the public. The number of women dying from illegal abortions was around 200-250 annually. The figure we constantly fed to the media was 10,000. These false figures took root in the consciousness of Americans, convincing many that we needed to crack the abortion law."[21]

After the 1973 US Supreme Court decision commonly referred to as *Roe vs Wade*, which allowed unlimited access to abortion, Nathanson says his group was inundated with requests for abortion:

> To that end, I set up a clinic, the Center for Reproductive and Sexual Health (CRASH), which operated in the east side of Manhattan. It had 10 operating rooms, 35 doctors, 85 nurses. It operated seven days a week, from 8 am to midnight. We did 120 abortions every day in that clinic. At the end of the two years that I was the director, we had

done 60,000 abortions. I myself, with my own hands, have done 5,000 abortions. I have supervised another 10,000 that residents have done under my direction. So I have 75,000 abortions in my life.[22]

How someone at the centre of the "pro-choice" movement could have found his way out of such a mind set to anything remotely connected with Catholicism is hard to imagine. Bernard Nathanson documents his inner journey out of the abortion industry in his autobiography *The Hand of God: A Journey from Death to Life by the Abortion Doctor Who Changed His Mind* (1996) which is a fascinating testimony of someone who found his way from the deepest darkness to authenticity and life.

The inner changes began to come for him in the 1970s with the growth of doubts about what he was doing. These arose largely from the arrival of ultrasound, showing real live unborn human beings on TV screens before him. After gazing at the movements of the unborn child, despite all he had formerly believed and done, he came to realise that the unborn child is a member of the human community. He argues this evidence alone should be enough to convince those who look at such screens. Thus his movement was more towards a realisation of the value of each human life, before his conversion to any religious faith.

At this time of inner questioning and prior to his conversion, there were difficulties within his personal life, a series of tragedies that led him to think of the ultimate dimensions of life and death. Nathanson married four times, his first three marriages ending in divorce. There had been a history of suicide in his family: his paternal grandfather had committed suicide, as had his father's sister; and Nathanson himself did contemplate it. He writes of this inner unease and of often waking in the middle of the night:

... staring into the darkness and hoping (but not praying yet) for a message to flare forth acquitting me before some invisible jury.[23]

When, finally after long soul searching and being confronted with the reality of the living child in the new ultrasound pictures before him, he decided to do no more abortions. He describes his existential dilemma as he wondered whether or not to commit suicide following realisation that he had killed so many innocent children. He writes of himself at this stage when he was trying to come to terms with what he did:

> Like the diagnostician I was trained to be, I commenced to analyse the patient's humours, the patient being myself. I determined that I was suffering from an affliction of the spirit; the disorder had arisen, at least in part, from an excess of existential freedom, and this had created a penumbral despair. I had been cast adrift in a limitless sea of sensual freedom – no sextant, no compass, no charts, simply the dimly apprehended stars of the mores of society (a chimpanzee could be trained to do as well, a minimalist concept of justice, and a stultified sense of decency). I required not a cure but a healing. I had performed many thousands of abortions on innocent human beings.[24]

Having tried alcohol, tranquillisers, self-help books, counselling and psychoanalysis up to this point, he finally found a secure starting point for his journey in being honest with himself, in realising he despised himself for what he had done. He thought, as had Santayana, that the only true dignity of man is in his capacity to despise himself. He had hardly begun a serious self examination but he was able to observe:

> I knew that the primary illness is the severing of the links between sin and fault, between ethically corrupt action and the cost. There had been no concrete cost to my corrupt action, only behavioural exegesis and that would not do.

I needed to be disciplined and educated. I had become as Hannah Arendt had described Eichmann: a collection of functions rather than an accountable human being.[25]

His harrowing confrontation with what he had done and his contemplation of what he should do, led him to think that he would do more for others if he gave witness to the truth of what he had done. In the 1980s he directed and narrated a film entitled *The Silent Scream* which described what occurred in an abortion, in very quiet factual terms, in cooperation with the National Right to Life Committee. The film itself had an extraordinary influence around the globe, having been translated into dozens of languages.

Nathanson's personal journey through suffering took a long time. But the labyrinth of thought and questioning brought him back to a belief in God, through one of those strange coincidences that occur in some lives – or should we say, rather, there are no coincidences? He met a priest with whom he talked for several years. There was no sudden blinding epiphany for him but a long process of questioning, discussion, discernment and gradual movement towards the realisation that there was a God and that we are not alone in the universe. He finally converted to Catholicism in 1996. He describes being moved by the story of a man dying from cancer who was asked by a passer-by what he was praying for so constantly. "It isn't for anything", the patient replied. "It mainly reminds me that we are not alone." Nathanson, after leaving a hell akin to Dante's inferno, realised that he was not alone and says of his epic inner journey at the conclusion of his book:

> It has been my fate to wander the globe in search of the One without Whom I am doomed, but now I seize the hem of His robe in desperation, in terror, in celestial access to the purest need I have ever known.[26]

On the day he made his first confession, Nathanson recalls the lights of the church going out and rather than reading an account of his sins from a prepared sheet of paper he spoke from memory to the priest in the darkness surrounding him. This day was a literal coming out from darkness into the light, mirroring his inner journey.

The spiritual dimension is the only one that could contain Nathanson's grief and self-horror. The realisation that God's mercy was greater than anything he had done saved him from self-destruction. His own public witness to his journey "out of hell" is an intelligent detailed account that resonates with many other doctors caught in this industry and now is of inestimable help to them. Nathanson, with the other doctors who have left the abortion industry in recent years, are pioneers within the medical profession and their conversions are astounding testimony to the strength of the spirit in a secular social context hostile to such conversions. They have stood up to the prevailing status quo at great personal cost to themselves and to great effect in the extent of their influence on others. They are truly extraordinary witnesses to the power of love and life which conquers all.

After giving constant witness to his journey out of darkness to his Catholic faith, travelling around the world to do so, Nathanson died of cancer in New York on 21 February 2011 at the age of 84. In the course of history, Nathanson's conversion occupies a most important historic place in humanity's attempt to counter the pro-choice views. It is a sign of contradiction which restores dignity to the profession which he finally realised should be devoted to saving lives. Most of all, his own account of his conversion is a moving personal witness of a person who sought light in the depths of the darkest places, who sought to touch the mystery of the Creator of life, and who sought the eternal truths and found them. It echoes in some way the final lines of G.K. Chesterton's poem "The Convert":

The sages have a hundred maps to give
That trace their crawling cosmos like a tree,
They rattle reason out through many a sieve
That stores the sand and lets the gold go free:
And all these things are less than dust to me
Because my name is Lazarus and I live.

21

From Judaism to Catholicism: Tom Leopold tells his story

Tom Leopold is a comedy writer who lives in New York City with his lovely wife Barbara and their two daughters. He has given kind permission (as has the editor of the 'Why I'm Catholic' website) for his conversion story to be told here.

My name is Tom Leopold and I'm a comedy writer (*Seinfeld, Cheers, Will and Grace* ...). I am a Jewish comedy writer, although I always felt saying that was kind of redundant. So much of my humor – practically all of it I suppose – comes from who my people are, what they've been through and how they were able to turn it all on its head and find the funny side, even and especially if there was none to find.

I know it sounds odd, but I always liked Jesus. I was never "deep" enough to wrestle with the concept of his being the son of God. For me he had this James Dean-Bob Dylan-daring rebel-hero "thing" about him. Once in a while, I did wonder, had I been nearby when Jesus walked among us, would I have had seen him for who he said he was? And, if so, would I have had the courage to say, "Hey, everybody says we're waiting on the Messiah. Well, the 'wait' is over!" Fast forward 2,000 years later and I'd follow Jesus anywhere if he'd have me.

Come Easter I'll still be a comedy writer, but a Catholic one. I consider my upcoming baptism a blessing. One that ranks right up there with the day I met my wife or the birth of our two daughters, to say nothing of having the good fortune to have made a living in a business that I love.

So here is a flashback of how I became Catholic.

We're a couple of years into my youngest daughter's life-threatening eating disorder. It also happens to be Christmas Eve and our girl is under doctors' care at still another rehab centre. This one is in the Arizona desert. By the time we had come to this point our ravaged little 14-year-old had been too ill to attend any but three weeks of her ninth grade school year, she had spent days locked in a psych ward, and both she and I were nearly run over by a cab as I tried to catch up to her after she'd bolted from a doctor's office.

So, we're in the desert, it's Christmas Eve and my wife, our oldest girl (17) and I are decorating our hotel room with Christmas stuff from the only store still open in the little desert town, the Dollar Store. We are all Jewish, but for some reason we've always celebrated Christmas too. There was something kind of sacred about the silly little tree we bought ... It reminded me of the tree Charlie Brown dragged back to his gang.

The doctors would only let us have our daughter for Christmas Day, so the three of us went to bed early, each trying not to let the others know how sad we were that one of us was missing. Lying there in the dark that night was the closest I have ever come to breaking – not breaking down, breaking! It's a whole lot easier to hold your heart together when it's you who does the suffering, but when it's your child and nobody can fix her ... Well, it would take more than a comedy writer to say it how it feels.

I was praying before the thought dawned on me that I was praying. Maybe begging is the better word ... "Please God, give me even the smallest sign you're up there, I just can't make it alone!"

The next morning we'd arranged for our girls to go horseback riding, and my wife and I took a walk in the desert. Out of nowhere this cool old guy drives up on a motorcycle he made himself ... It had antlers for handlebars and the guy looked like the old Marine that he turned out to be. He skidded up next to us, practically popping a wheelie, and started talking. I'm a New Yorker, so I just figured he was just one more weirdo ... But the guy had this great intensity and a mysterious charisma.

He started a long monologue about how he was once married to a woman named "Shepard" and how his present wife brought him to Christ at the age of 33, and all the while he keeps nodding his head towards me and saying to my wife "This one knows what I'm talking about!"

Here we were, on Christmas morning in the desert, and this odd old character is throwing the word "Shepard" around along with the number 33. "Wasn't Jesus a 'Shepard' to his flock and wasn't he 33 when he was crucified and isn't this day, his birthday?!" As I'm thinking of this, the old guy keeps telling my wife that I know what he means! And the weird thing is I do, kind of, know what he means! Not what he's saying but what he means ...

My cell phone rings. It's our kids. They're through with their ride. Without even knowing who's on the other end of the phone our desert prophet says, "Hang up, they're fine!" I hung up. After the exhaustion of all we'd been through, it felt nice to be, well, led!

He finally stops talking, guns his engine and peels off only to stop a few yards away, turn back to me and say in a voice somewhere below a whisper and above mental telepathy that "God is watching you!" It wasn't a threat, it was a reassurance.

There were more things like that. Coincidences? I no longer think so. But the biggest and most rewarding was the day I ran into Father Jonathan Morris.

Thirty-eight years ago I went to a psychic down in Nolita (North of Little Italy) who pretty much predicted my entire career path ... I wasn't even a writer at the time. Out of the blue I had this idea to reconnect with him and, to my amazement, he remembered me right away. Our daughter had got a little better after her last treatment but was falling back again even though she was now strong enough to attend school. I thought I'd go visit Frank (my old psychic) just to check in and tell him how right he had been about all that's happened to me and to ask if he saw a recovery for our daughter. Frank told me to bring her to him. A few days later we did. Walking up the steps to Frank's townhouse, a car pulls up right in front of us and out steps Father Jonathan Morris. I recognised him from a picture in his book, *The Promise*. The book dealt with grief and I was getting a great deal of comfort from it. Suddenly the very same, kind, face was right before me.

"Are you Father Morris?"

He nodded.

"Your book is on my bed stand."

He had already started towards me. He had his hand out.

Why I said what I said next I will never know.

" Father, do you think you might have a few minutes to talk to me sometime?"

I had seen and admired Father Morris many times on television but thought he lived in Rome. He smiled, holding on to my hand and said: "You can find me right here." He turned and pointed to Old Saint Patrick's Church. It was as if I hadn't even seen the church until he pointed to it. He had just started as parochial vicar there ... True to his word he found time for me and room for my family in his prayers. He even met with our daughter.

I don't think there's room now to describe all I found "right here" at Old Saint Pat's. The minute Father Morris took my hand I knew I'd be a follower of Christ. Does my daughter still suffer? She does, we all still do, but now I feel the Lord's grace. We are not alone.

22

From the New Age to Catholicism

Moira Noonan was deeply into New Age and occult practices for many years before she converted to Catholicism. The story of her exit from the New Age is recounted in various places, most importantly her autobiography Ransomed from Darkness *(2009). The following recounts her story in briefer form and highlights some of the salient aspects of her journey. Her journey has touched many involved in the New Age with its invitation to consider what the New Age 'beliefs' really are. Moira is a clear, reasoning and kind voice reaching out to an age permeated with New Age ideas.*

Moira Noonan was born in the United States. She was baptised and had some rudimentary Catholic instruction in a Catholic primary school in Detroit but this rapidly dissipated and was forgotten as she grew up attending other schools. She attended a boarding school MacDuffie School for Girls in Springfield, Massachusetts, where she came under the influence of a teacher who was married to a Hindu and who opened the world of Eastern religions and enlightenment to her. She was receptive to New Age ideas. Later at college she furthered her interest and of this time she says:

> It is a common belief among New-Agers that follow Gurus that a Guru needs to be alive in order to help you. So on the college campus I attended, I was highly influenced by the Rashneesh movement. This movement really took off and their Guru eventually moved from India to the West Coast in the US to be with all of the young followers.[27]

In the mid-'70s Noonan graduated from university and obtained a publishing job in Hawaii and focused on her career. It was at this point in her life that she had an experience that well and truly catapulted her into the New Age. She had a bad car accident which resulted in her being in chronic pain and she was sent to La Crosse, Wisconsin, for some therapy which involved New Age thought deriving from theosophy and Christian Science. She states:

> The treatment offered was based entirely on "New Thought." New Thought was articulated in mid-19th century America by Phineas Quimby, a faith healer and medium who made a disciple of Mary Baker Eddy when he treated her for back pain. After Quimby died, Mrs Eddy amplified the ideas she had absorbed from him and others and expressed them in her own writings as Christian Science. International Religious Science, another outgrowth of the movement, was founded in the early 20th century by Ernest Holmes, author of *The Science of Mind*.

This immersion in New Age thought led her to develop the interest in fundamental new age ideas such as reincarnation, consciousness altering practices, particularly certain types of hypnosis. Noonan writes:

> This system of thought captured me through the interest I had developed in reincarnation when I was in high school. It never gave me the answers I sought, but the expectation of fulfilment, never satisfied but always promised, impelled me on to ten more years pursuing the New Age. Some patients stayed at the pain clinic for months, and many came back to have the hypnotic effect reinforced. But after a month, I no longer felt unmanageable pain, and I didn't need pain pills. That was the effect of hypnotic suggestion, not a physical healing. To stay well, I would have to keep doing self-hypnosis.

Noonan became increasingly drawn into New Age finding it seductive to hear that each person is "the ultimate power and moral authority". She delved into the Human Potential Movement, by way of Werner Erhard's "est," a programme later renamed the Forum and still later called Transformational Technologies, Inc. She tried Silva Mind Control and became involved in the work *A Course in Miracles*, which became such an international phenomenon at the time drawing in people with half formed notions of what the spiritual life entailed. She noted that this New Age publication was on offer in various Christian churches. Purporting to be "Christian" it obfuscated fundamental Christian beliefs as she explains:

> *A Course in Miracles* uses a vocabulary to indicate that its spirit-author is Jesus, bringing a new Revelation to "purify" the teachings of Christianity that are "His old Revelation." The "miracles" referred to in the title are not supernatural interventions in the natural order, but products of corrected thinking, as in other New Thought systems. The Course was published in 1976, and study groups began using it in New Age churches around the United States. Its success owes a good deal to Marianne Williamson, who discovered it at the West.

Noonan further explains that the New Age is like a never-ending road leading on to never-ending experimentation and "knowledge" considered to be of crucial importance to development in the inner life. She was drawn into theosophical thinking which seeks to draw its practitioners to a higher state of consciousness. Much of theosophy is allied with Eastern religions, particularly Buddhism and Hinduism. Thus she studied the ideas they expounded of "progressive spiritual evolution" by which means she could escape her bad karma from the "wheel of reincarnation" and become a more evolved person, one with the Universal Mind. In way she was inducted into the Monist (everything is god) belief of Eastern thought. She studied people who had attained to a higher state of being – the "Ascended Masters" who were considered the spiritual leaders who rule planet Earth and help others to "get there". As she explains:

> In standard theosophical theory and in interpretations of Elizabeth Clare Prophet (Church Universal and Triumphant), Alice Bailey (New Group of World Servers), and similar sects, Jesus is considered one of the Ascended Masters – but not superior to Buddha, St Germain, Kuthumi, El Morya or Maitreya.

Thus Noonan was not averse to hearing about Jesus but he was no different from any other Ascended Master of whom there were ever increasing numbers. The term "Christ consciousness" simply referred to a higher state of consciousness and awareness of the new order into which the world is evolving, a view commonly held by followers of the New Age, whatever their proclivities and particular interests. Noonan also explores Shamanism and other ancient pagan ways of thought and American Medicine Cards which are like Tarot cards but using American Indian symbolism.

Noonan was married in 1983 in an Episcopal church in Seattle and she recalls that the officiating clergyman was a former Catholic priest who had left the priesthood to marry a former nun. She separated from her husband in 1991 and by that time had a daughter Malia. When she was pregnant with her daughter Noonan recalls that she went on holiday to Europe with her mother. While in Paris, her mother asked her daughter to come into the Basilica of Sacre Coeur where they stayed for Mass. Noonan recalls looking at the votive candles and statues, especially one of the Virgin Mary, and her actions seem inexplicable to her in retrospect.

> Leaving my mother behind in the pew, I went over to the

shrine, lit a candle, and consecrated my unborn baby to the Virgin Mary. "Blessed Mother, this is your child." I whispered. "I give this child to you." When our daughter was born, I called her Malia, the Hawaiian form of "Mary."

This action did not signal any exit from the New Age, however, for Noonan then returned to Southern California where she enrolled in the North County Church of Religious Science in order to "minister" New Age ideas to others. It was what she calls an even "more sophisticated brainwashing" than she had encountered previously leading her from what she called self-confidence to "self-idolatry". She then graduated as a New Age professional initially becoming a prayer practitioner:

> In my first venture as a New Age professional, I became a "prayer practitioner" at the Seaside Church of Religious Science, in Del Mar, where my stipends came from client donations to the church. My work had nothing to do with God or prayer as Catholics use those terms. Prayer practitioners use their "Christ consciousness" to help people "manifest" (i.e., obtain) what they desire by commanding the universal Mind as a magician would command a genie, rather than beseeching God's help.

Underlying this "prayer" was the notion that any person could access and obtain whatever he/she wanted through "treatments" (i.e., prayer sessions) because each person was divine and could tap into the divine will. This was diametrically opposed to any notion of Christian prayer in which the created being prays to the uncreated God. As she puts it: "The essence of the New Age teachings is to manifest into human experience what they consider to be the divine will" because they think that we are all "gods".[28]

This prayer practitioner work inspired her to seek to do some form of healing and counselling work with others and this led her to Reiki:

> I became a Reiki Master healer and teacher. Reiki calls on spirit guides of fallen angels (demons) to transmit healing energy through touch or by directed thought, even from a distance. A Reiki Master in Ohio might direct healing energy to a patient in Hawaii – or back into the past or forward into the future. I took training classes from Barbara Brennan, founder and director of the Hands of Light School of Healing in New York. Hands of Light healing is similar to Reiki, but focuses on diagnosing and treating the "aura" or energy field that is believed to surround and flow through all living things, and is visible to clairvoyants.

She grew proficient at Reiki and even became a master practitioner at it. At the same time, in the way that "enough is never enough" Noonan also did psychic training and says this is not something to be taken lightly. She really did have contact with spirits and really did communicate with them:

> When I told people I saw something, like their childhood experiences, I did see them. I could sit down beside a stranger and see his past life unreel like a movie. Sometimes I could converse with the people I was seeing. But like other clairvoyant channelers, I couldn't sleep at night because the "messages" demanding attention in my mind became a torment, and I could not turn them off.

Noonan went into many different types of New Age practices including Eriksonian hypnotherapy and Anthony Robbins Neurolinguistic Programming. She says of Eriksonian therapy that it is not a scientific procedure as is often assumed. She learned that it covered a myriad of complex techniques including "the New Age spectrum, from simple insights into psychology to shamanism, trance mediumship, Jungian psychology, Mind Control, 'mind mapping', and past-life regression." She became a certified Ericksonian hypnotherapist and was so immersed in its techniques that she noticed strange things happening to her mind, that she developed a dependence on self-hypnosis which in turn weakened her exercise of will power. She was no longer in control of her free will, as happens to many who engage in consciousness altering practices, and at a subtle level she knew something was happening to her that was not altogether for the good.

It was at this time that she chanced to pick up a magazine with an article by a New Age practitioner who had visited Medjugorje, Sondra Ray. Ray said that she was convinced that "Mary" was a goddess come down to meet the earth goddess Gaia. Noonan was so entranced with the story that she could not put it down and kept thinking of "Our Lady". This led her to try to re-engage with some remnants of her Catholic infancy. Her daughter Malia had said on several occasions that she did not want to go to the New Age "church" at which her mother was "ministering". Noonan had allowed her to go to a Lutheran Sunday school as a neighbour offered to take her there. But now, with this thinking about "Our Lady" and memories of shards of Catholicism returning to her she wanted her daughter to also connect with it in some way. She recalls;

> I called a nearby Catholic parish (St John the Evangelist in Encinitas), and told the religious ed. coordinator, Cindy Combs, about our tangled situation. I said I was a New Age minister at the Church of Religious Science, but I really wanted my daughter to make her First Communion in the Catholic Church. With great kindness, Cindy took Malia under her wing and enrolled her in the Monday night CCD programme.

While Malia received Catholic instruction, she continued to attend Lutheran Sunday school. She recalled later that this experience had been a kind of bridge to Christianity and she was very grateful to the neighbour who took her there. Noonan remembers that at this time her grandmother died and bequeathed to her a miraculous medal and that she started to say the *Memorare* to St Bernard printed on the sheet which came with the medal. She pinpoints this moment as the beginning of her conversion. But there was still a long way to go even though she was praying a Catholic prayer and fascinated by the reported apparitions in Medjugorje. She heard some people interviewed on the *Joan Rivers Show* one night which aroused her interest in the Charismatic movement and she found herself going to a centre:

> We found the address of a "Catholic Charismatic Center" in La Jolla. When we called and asked whether anyone there could tell us about the apparitions, and the possibility of visiting Medjugorje as tourists, we were told, "Come right over. A speaker is going to talk about it this very day." We listened eagerly to what the speakers said about the apparitions, and bought a beautiful Medjugorje poster. But when the talks ended, and they invited us to stay on for a Bible study, we said, "No, thank you." For years, we had been studying the Bible "metaphysically," and we thought we knew more about it than they did. So we decided to go off by ourselves and do some crystal work instead.

As she and her friend Ciera were leaving Noonan recalls that she met Beverly Nelson, a lay missionary with Mother Teresa's Missionaries of Charity. Beverly proved to be an important guide in my journey back to the faith. She said that it was not necessary to go to Medjugorje to experience the love of Our Lady and that there were other apparitions she could read about closer to home. They tried to use crystal clairvoyancy to lead them to an apparition but at that moment something unusual happened to Noonan. She said that she could see a rosary in the palm of her hand and that an internal voice was saying "pray the rosary". Noonan immediately said to her friend that they had to pray this prayer and they did. They decided to pursue the story of apparitions in Scottsdale but instead found themselves attracted to going to a Catholic church in Scottsdale instead. There they prayed 15 decades of the rosary and attended a healing Mass. Noonan recalls:

> At Communion time, I had the audacity to go forward and receive Our Lord unworthily. Instantly, with scalding conviction, I recognised my sinfulness and my desperate need for Confession. When the Mass ended, I rushed to the sacristy and asked to speak to a priest. "Father has already left," an altar boy said. "You might be able to catch him in the parking lot if you hurry." So I dashed out the door and searched the parking lot for the priest. When I found him, he was getting ready to leave. "Father, I've got to make a confession really fast!" I said to him. So right there, standing in the lot beside his car, he heard my 20-year confession.

Noonan continued to pray the rosary and then found a place to receive Catholic instruction in San Diego. She decided to do this at a place called the "Prince of Peace" abbey as she was drawn to its name, saying that a friend informed her "That's a name for Jesus," he said, "You surely must have learned that in Sunday school or somewhere!" But I hadn't, or if I had I could not remember it. I went into the chapel and prayed without moving for two hours. "Oh Jesus," I said, "If you are the Prince of Peace, I really need you, because no one has been able to give me peace."

The reason that Noonan, despite her newly found prayers and love of Catholicism could find no peace, was that she was still held in thrall by the clairvoyant visions and powers with which she had previously engaged. She said: "My head was like a metro train station at rush hour, and I could not sleep, because the clairvoyant visions would not leave me alone." She saw God's providence in leading her to the Prince of Peace Abbey as there was a priest there familiar with Eastern religions and the type of influences Noonan had had in her life. He realised she was in bondage to ideas such as reincarnation and other deep-seated spiritualist powers but with repeated confessions, healing prayer and reception of the sacraments the bondage was loosened. This was a slow process but the happiest journey of her life. She is now a fervent Catholic and has been able to get through to others embroiled in New Age practices and ideas. In this way Noonan has put her sufferings and experiences to good use and brought many of her New Age friends into the Church.

23

JoAnna, a mother of four, tells her story

JoAnna is married and has four children. This is her story as a lifelong member of the Lutheran Church to Catholicism. With grateful acknowledgement to JoAnna and to the site 'Why I'm Catholic'.[29] JoAnna also has her own website for Catholic mothers called 'A Star of Hope' located at http://a-star-of-hope.blogspot.com.au/

I was born to lifelong Lutherans (ELCA – Evangelic Lutheran Church in America) who, of course, baptised all their kids Lutheran. I was baptised on 28 December 1980, a date that I realised, soon after my conversion, was the Feast of the Holy Innocents. I sometimes wonder why I wasn't baptised sooner given that I was born six weeks prematurely, but I suppose that in Lutheran circles baptism isn't considered crucial for newborns, even premature ones.

At any rate, I was raised in a Lutheran home. My parents took us to church and Sunday school regularly, a fact for which I am grateful. Religion was sometimes discussed in our home but mostly in response to questions I posed after reading the Bible (which I did at an early age) or watching movies about Jesus. It was never a topic I remember my parents initiating or even discussing in detail (either with us or with each other). My feeling all through childhood was that church and religion were Sunday activities. That's not to say that my parents were nominally religious – it's just that God, Jesus, religion, etc, didn't seem to play that large a part in our day-to-day lives. That's just my perception, looking back after many years.

I was confirmed in the ELCA in 1994, I believe. I remember

that as part of one of the Confirmation classes, we were required to memorise and recite a part of the Small Catechism. I was assigned the Last Supper discourse ("this is my body, given for you ...") and I remember being very pleased to have that particular part. Even then I considered Communion to be pretty special. During this time period, my parents were going through a bitter divorce, and my faith was my solace.

In 1999, I went off to college at the University of Wyoming. I began attending a Lutheran church close to campus in Laramie, and also began attending a Christian group on campus called Chi Alpha, run by the Assembly of God Church (i.e., fundamentalist). There was no conflict between the two; theology was never really discussed or brought up. I met many fantastic friends through Chi Alpha, including my best friend and former roommate Rose. It was a wonderful college experience. I didn't get too terribly involved with my Laramie ELCA church; I mainly attended because it reminded me of home.

In 2000, at the end of my sophomore year, I met my future husband, Collin, online; in 2001 we were married and I moved to Minneapolis, transferring to the University of Minnesota-Twin Cities. I remember being pleased to learn that Collin was, like me, a lifelong member of the ELCA. Although he'd fallen away from Christianity for a time as a teenager, a class he took in college called "The Writings of C.S. Lewis" brought him back and caused him to take his faith more seriously. We were married in Our Savior's Lutheran Church, the same church where I'd been confirmed, on 1 September 2001.

Fast forward a few years ... one day, I think it was in early January 2003, Collin surprised me with the announcement that he'd been doing a lot of thinking, research, and praying, and he felt God was leading him to convert to the Catholic Church. I was aghast at the very idea.

As it turned out, Collin had been having a lot of theological discussions with his best friend, who's Catholic, and he had come to the conclusion that the Catholic Church was the only one with the fullness of Truth. I disagreed, but after a few weeks of talking about the issue, I agreed to go to RCIA with him. I thought that if I was going to be raising our potential kids Catholic, then I should know more about the Faith. At the time I started RCIA, I had no intention of converting.

I have to admit that things had been bothering me about the ELCA for a while prior to Collin's announcement. For example, I found out that the ELCA's health care plan for its employees (e.g., its ministers) paid for abortion. I found that disturbing, as I've always been staunchly pro-life ... and then when I read ELCA's actual statement on abortion which seemed rather wishy-washy to me. I've since written an article for the Catholic Phoenix blog going into what exactly I found so disturbing about the ELCA's stance on abortion.

While in RCIA I was confronted with questions I hadn't really thought about before.

First and foremost was the sola scriptura issue. The Catholic Church's authority is like a three-legged stool, with Scripture, Sacred Tradition, and the Magisterium all having equal weight. Protestant traditions all go by the Bible alone. However, when it comes down to it, this doesn't really make sense. After all, Jesus spoke pretty clearly about being a unified Church, but there are 5,000+ Protestant churches that all claim to go by the Bible alone. Who is right? They can't all be right. Would Jesus really leave His Church in such confusion?

Also, the doctrine of sola scriptura is not actually found in the Bible. Nowhere does Jesus or any of the Apostles, or St Paul, say that we should only follow the Scriptures. We are told that the Scriptures are good, profitable, etc, but we are never told they are the sole rule of faith. St Peter warns against private interpretation of the Scriptures, a cornerstone of the Protestant faith, and St Paul tells Timothy to follow the traditions he'd been taught! I had never been faced with these apparent contractions before.

Once I concluded that sola scriptura was false, that begged the question: do Christians have an authority on Earth, one that interprets God's Word in light of our modern times and shepherds Christ's flock?

If you read the early Church fathers, they were remarkably Catholic. They believed in the perpetual virginity of Mary, the transubstantiation of the Eucharist, and so on. The Protestant argument seems to be that the Catholic Church eventually corrupted Christianity and the Protestant reformation put it back on track. But if the Church from its earliest days was Catholic, could it really have been corrupted so soon? It didn't seem logical that God would put His Church in human hands, only to see it go corrupt before two generations after Christ.

Also, the Bible wasn't even compiled until around AD 400. If we were supposed to go by the Bible alone, what did the earliest Christians do? Moreover, it was the Catholic Church that compiled and established the canon of books of the Bible, so it didn't make sense to me that Protestants trusted the Church to compile an inspired and inerrant Bible, but not to be authoritative in any other way.

Then I started to read more about the Church's claim to authority; that is, that the Pope is the successor of Peter, and it just made sense to me that Jesus would establish an earthly Church with an earthly successor to guide His flock. In addition to giving Peter the keys of the kingdom (Matthew 16:18-20), He even told Peter three times to feed His sheep (John 21:15-17) – not any of the other apostles, but Peter alone.

Once I began to believe that the Pope was the successor of Peter, the whole papal infallibility concept made more sense, and once that fell into place, so did everything else (the Eucharist, Mary, etc). I figured that if Jesus had given the Church authority to teach, then I should follow those teachings – otherwise, I wasn't really following Jesus to the best of my ability.

I also read a lot of conversion stories about Protestants who became Catholic, such as Scott Hahn's *Rome Sweet Home* and Jimmy Akin's conversion story. Also helpful was Patrick Madrid's *Surprised by Truth* series. After my conversion I discovered Mark Shea's books, which are a must-read for anyone considering Catholicism – especially *By What Authority? An Evangelical Discovers Catholic Tradition.* I also spent a lot of time on the Catholic Answers forums, talking with other Catholics about the Catholic Church.

Another turning point in my conversion was realising the beauty of the Mass. When I first started attending Mass (very reluctantly), I thought it was staid and boring. Then came Holy Week. I was struck by how intense the services were, how much they focused on Christ and His passion. We went to the Easter Vigil Mass at the Basilica of St Mary, and it literally changed my mind about the Mass overnight. The sheer beauty that overwhelmed the senses as I heard the readings and heard the music and smelled the incense – the pure joy that seemed to emanate from the very stones as the lights of the Basilica were thrown on full force after the darkness of Good Friday – the happiness of the newly baptised – well, it was an experience, and I began to see the Mass in a whole new light.

Collin and I were confirmed into the Catholic Church on 29 May 2003. We were originally scheduled to be confirmed at Pentecost, which was that Sunday, but I had just graduated from college two weeks before and we'd made plans to move out of state that weekend, so the priest graciously agreed to confirm us on a Thursday daily Mass instead. I hope the people who attended that particular daily Mass were pleasantly surprised to be present at a confirmation! I took a confirmation name, Anne, because St Anne is the patron saint of motherhood and I knew it was my vocation to some day be a mother. (As it turned out, our daughter Elanor was baptised into the Catholic Church almost exactly two years later, on 28 May 2005.)

Through our Catholic faith we also discovered the joys of Natural Family Planning and have been using it to both achieve and postpone pregnancy since 2003. In addition to our oldest daughter born in January 2005, we've conceived an additional five children, two of whom we lost to miscarriage.

Our home church is the Basilica of St Mary in downtown Minneapolis, MN. It is an incredible church, full of peace and beauty. The reason we chose it was quite simple – it was within walking distance of our apartment; actually, the walk was the perfect amount of time needed to say a rosary. As Collin chose that apartment before he'd even considered looking into the Catholic Church, God provided him (and me) the perfect church home even before we knew we'd need one!

24

A Hindu couple joins the Catholic Church

In the conversion story of Uma and Kumar, dreams play a part, as they sometimes do, in the journeys of those who have come into the Church. This following account is printed with kind permission from the Arlington Catholic Herald, *from the Diocese of Arlington, Virginia (USA).*

It was three years ago when Uma Krishnan, a devout Hindu, says she first dreamed of the Virgin Mary. It was January 2006 and she was living in Singapore with her husband, Kumar, and her son, Karthi. In her dream she saw a "very humble lady" surrounded by candles.

She and Kumar knew the lady in Uma's dreams was not a Hindu god. They knew little of Christianity, but they thought this lady might be the Blessed Mother. Still, because they came from a long tradition of Hinduism in India, they didn't give the dream much thought.

Later that year Kumar got a job that took him to San Diego. A few months later, he found a new job in McLean. Uma and Karthi joined him that December.

Then in April, Uma began to have more dreams of Mary.

One night she dreamed she was walking into a church she'd never seen before. Once inside, she turned right and found a little room where there were red candles and a statue of Mary.

The second night, she was in the same room, but this time she saw a big cross made of palm leaves.

Another night, she dreamed she was in a boat. On her right was a black woman with dark hair and on her left, a lady wearing a blue scarf and holding a Bible. The woman in blue showed Uma some verses to read to make her worries disappear. In her dream, Uma read the Bible verses and both women disappeared.

Uma and Kumar talked about the dreams and, by the fourth night, they decided to visit a church to see what was happening.

Kumar typed "St Mary Church Fairfax" into Google and entered the address from the first result into his GPS device. The address was for St Mary of Sorrows Church in Fairfax.

When they got to the church, Uma was shocked. On the outside, it looked just like the church she had dreamed about the first night. When they went inside and turned right, there was a small chapel with red votive candles, a statue of Mary and a cross. It was just like her dreams. Uma started to cry.

"The moment was so touching," Kumar said. "We were not even Christians and we were not even worshipping when we got such a thing. We were Hindus and we didn't exactly know how to pray, but we just sat there and said, 'Thank you. Thank you for all these visions and thank you for bringing us here. We don't know what to do, you tell us, you guide us, show us what has to be done'."

After the first visit to the church, a few days passed and Uma and Kumar didn't return. Instead, they went to their Hindu temple.

Uma had another dream. She saw the statue of Mary on the outside wall of the church. Mary's arms were out and there was a bright light coming from behind. In Uma's mind, the statue seemed to be saying, "Come back to me."

When Uma told Kumar, they decided to go to St Mary of Sorrows that day. It was a Wednesday, and this time, they went into the main meeting room, where the Charismatic Prayer Group gathered. They shared their story and prayed with them.

After that, Uma and Kumar began to attend Mass and the Charismatic Prayer Group every week.

Uma's dreams continued, but the couple also started experiencing strange "spiritual disturbances". Uma would have nightmares, and during the day, alone at home, she would hear strange laughing, heavy breathing or footsteps. Sometimes she would feel a pressure on her neck and would have trouble breathing.

The disturbances were so bad that Uma was afraid to be alone. Kumar would drop her off at St Mary of Sorrows when he went to work in the morning and she would stay at the church all day.

Frightened, Uma and Kumar talked to Father Stefan Starzynski, St Mary of Sorrows parochial vicar.

Starzynski told them the disturbances might be coming because they were moving away from Hinduism. He told them not to worry and that they'd be OK if they just went toward the one, true God.

"Even as Hindus they were coming to the prayer groups and the healing Masses and praying the rosary every day, so I think something was trying to stop them from entering the Faith fully," Father Starzynski said.

Kumar and Uma decided to get rid of all of their Hindu belongings and devote themselves entirely to Catholicism.

Because of their circumstances, the parish had a team of four parishioners teach the couple a condensed version of the traditional year long Rite of Christian Initiation for Adults programme. Uma and Kumar went to the programme every Saturday to learn about the sacraments and to discuss the Bible.

"It sounded like Mary was calling them to us and I felt like we had a responsibility to them," said Father Starzynski. "They told me they wanted to become Catholic and they were so excited and eager that I thought this was an opportunity to be flexible."

By the end of August 2007, the group decided the family was ready to become Catholic. On 12 September, Uma, Kumar and Karthi were baptised and the couple received the sacraments of confirmation, Communion and marriage.

In the days leading up to the ceremonies, Uma and Kumar felt they received lots of help from Mary.

Though they had a very limited budget and hardly any time to plan, Uma and Kumar wanted to have a nice wedding ceremony. They only had $400 to spend on a wedding dress for Uma, but their son found a perfect dress for $399.

Then, after deciding wedding photographers would be too expensive, a photographer from the parish offered his services for free.

Before the baptism and wedding day, Uma had another dream. This time Mary was standing outside the historic St Mary of Sorrows Church, with a big smile on her face. She was holding two wedding rings and three rosaries – red, orange and yellow.

The couple decided to use those colours in Uma's bouquet and on the wedding cake, all donated by fellow churchgoers.

On the actual day, the whole parish was invited to see Uma and Kumar receive the sacraments. A reception was held in the hall of the historic church, decorated with red, orange and yellow flowers.

"Even though we hadn't planned things, God had planned for us," Kumar said. "He planned everything so perfectly and he took care of everything, right down to the photographs. It was like he has predicted this marriage for us. We are so glad and so thankful and so lucky to be here."

Father Starzynski said Uma and Kumar's conversion story shows that God works in mysterious ways. He felt honoured that he could be there to help the family.

"I think it speaks to how beautifully God can work and does work," he said. "It makes you think, are we flexible enough to understand the ways God may work that are outside the box that we have constructed?"

Since they received the sacraments, Kumar and Uma say the disturbances and nightmares have stopped. Uma feels stronger and is able to stay home by herself with no fear.

"We feel like the Holy Spirit in her has just given her this total protection," Kumar said.

The couple says they are constantly impressed with the parish community.

"I feel like I've been wandering all over the place and that I've come home," Kumar said. "I never heard of such good people, such good Catholic people."

And through it all, Uma's dreams of Mary continue.

"Whether it's good or bad, we want to share them with everybody so everybody knows about it," Kumar said. "Some may take it badly, but we want to share it. We are very fortunate. I feel lucky, I feel honoured and I feel blessed."

Endnotes

1 With grateful acknowledgment to Katie. The above account of Katie's conversion appeared on the Catholic Archdiocese of Adelaide website. http://www.adelaide.catholic.org.au/our-faith/becoming-a-catholic (Accessed 2 July 2014).

2 R.J. Stove's story can be found on the *Why I'm Catholic* site under the title "Atheist Convert: R.J. Stove": http://whyimcatholic.com/index.php/conversion-stories/atheist-converts/item/96-atheist-convert-rj-stove (Accessed 7 July 2013). All quotations are from this site.

3 Ibid.

4 Ibid.

5 The entire conversion diary is available on: http://veritasvosliberabit70.blogspot.com.au// (Accessed 5 March 2012).

6 This letter and all subsequent personal correspondence were on site at time of publication: http://veritasvosliberabit70.blogspot.com.au/

7 One powerful example is David Horowitz's work *Radical Son: A Generational Odyssey*, USA: Touchstone Book, 1998.

8 Tony Abbott, *The Australian*, 15 June 2013. http://www.theaustralian.com.au/opinion/christopher-pearson-a-man-of-letters-who-opened-windows-on-the-world/story-e6frg6zo-1226664040227#sthash.6twOvDEk.dpuf (Accessed 31 September 2013).

9 Quoted in: Jacquelynne Wilcox, "Remembering Christopher Pearson", 11 June 2013, *Indaily*. http://indaily.com.au/news/2013/06/11/remembering-christopher-pearson/ (Accessed 20 October 2013)

10 Ibid.

11 Christopher Pearson, "No regrets about act of faith despite church's woeful state", *The Australian*, 5 September 2009. http://www.theaustralian.com.au/opinion/columnists/no-regrets-about-act-of-faith-despite-churchs-woeful-state/story-e6frg7ko-1225769660350 (Accessed 20 October 2013).

12 Ibid.

13 Ibid.

14 Wilcox, "Remembering Christopher Pearson."

15 Ibid.

16 Pearson, "No regrets about act of faith despite church's woeful state."

17 This account first appeared the *Catholic Answers Magazine* on the following site: http://www.catholic.com/magazine/articles/why-i-didn%E2%80%99t-convert-to-eastern-orthodoxy It has been reprinted with the kind permission of Father Brian Harrison and Karl Keating of Catholic Answers. (Accessed 14 February 2013).

18 Paul Williams gave his permission to use the account he has published on the following site: http://whyimcatholic.com/index.php/conversion-stories/buddhist-converts/65-buddhist-convert-paul-williams (Accessed 5 September 2013).

19 Paul Williams provides this addendum to his article for those wishing to follow up with further readings, with references given in the following manner. Some further reading on Buddhism and Catholicism by Paul Williams: *The Unexpected Way*, UK: Continuum, 2002; *Buddhism from a Catholic Perspective*, Catholic Truth Society, 2006; "Buddhism", in Gavin D'Costa (ed.) *The Catholic Church and the World Religions: A Theological and Phenomenological Account*, UK: Continuum, 2011.

20 "National Abortion Rights Action League Founder Reminisces": http://www.pregnantpause.org/abort/remember-naral.htm (Accessed 13 May 2012).

21 Ibid.

22 Ibid.

23 Bernard Nathanson, *The Hand of God: A Journey from Death to Life by the Abortion Doctor Who Changed His Mind*, Washington DC: Regnery Press, 1996, 188.

24 Ibid, 189.

25 Ibid, 189.

26 Ibid, 196.

27 Moira Noonan, "My Conversion Story": http://www.christendom-awake.org/pages/moira-noonan/conversion-story.htm (Accessed 9 April 2013).

28 Ibid. (Accessed 9 April 2013).

29 The site entitled "Why I'm Catholic" is: http://whyimcatholic.com

www.ingramcontent.com/pod-product-compliance
Lightning Source LLC
Chambersburg PA
CBHW032023230426
43671CB00005B/178